D0016149

HOW TO BE INVISIBLE

THOMAS DUNNE BOOKS
ST. MARTIN'S PRESS
NEW YORK

HOW
TO BE
INVISIBLE

A STEP-BY-STEP GUIDE TO PROTECTING YOUR ASSETS, YOUR IDENTITY, AND YOUR LIFE

J. J. LUNA

This publication is for informational purposes only and should not be used as a substitute for legal or other professional advice. If professional advice or other expert assistance is required, the services of a competent professional should be sought to address the particular circumstances involved.

THOMAS DUNNE BOOKS.
An imprint of St. Martin's Press.

HOW TO BE INVISIBLE. Copyright © 2000 by Editorial de Las Islas LC. All rights reserved. Printed in the United States of America. No part of this book may be used or reproduced in any manner whatsoever without written permission except in the case of brief quotations embodied in critical articles or reviews. For information, address St. Martin's Press, 175 Fifth Avenue, New York, N.Y. 10010.

www.stmartins.com

Book design by mspaceny/Maura Fadden Rosenthal

Library of Congress Cataloging-in-Publication Data

Luna, J. J.
    How to be invisible : a step-by-step guide to protecting your assets, your identity, and your life / J. J. Luna.
        p.   cm.
    ISBN 0-312-25250-1
    1. Privacy, Right of—United States. 2. Identification—United State. I. Title.

JC596.2.U5 L86 2000
323.44'8'0973—dc21

                                                            00-023903

10   9   8

A NOTE TO READERS

This book is sold with the understanding that it is not meant to offer or replace legal or investment advice. Laws vary—what is legal in one state may be illegal in another. Laws and procedures also change frequently, and are subject to different interpretations. Moreover, the general situation described in this book may not apply to your particular circumstances. Thus, no action recommended in this book should be taken without first obtaining advice and counsel of a trained legal professional.

This book is dedicated to an anonymous member of Spain's Secret Police. On January 27, 1960, during a brief encounter on a quiet back street in Santa Cruz de Tenerife, I asked him for advice on how best to avoid any problems in the land of Generalissimo Francisco Franco. The advice he gave me has served me well for forty years. He said there was only one way to avoid troubles with the authorities: "Make yourself invisible."

CONTENTS

HOW TO BE INVISIBLE

1

HOW THIS BOOK CAN MAKE YOU INVISIBLE

> *Governments keep a lot of secrets from their people . . .*
> *Why aren't the people in return allowed to keep secrets*
> *from the government?*
>
> —PHILIP ZIMMERMAN, DER SPIEGEL

Sometimes life has a way of appearing as nothing more than a string of minor and major disasters, a series of challenges that, when considered in their totality, can overwhelm even the most levelheaded of individuals. In fact, it's only prudent to prepare for the worst that life has to offer: thus, life insurance, home insurance, extra batteries, security systems, dead bolts, a little fire extinguisher in the kitchen, and on and on. However, there's one glaring omission in most people's planning, one gap in their vigilance which is potentially more devastating than if they went through life smoking in bed, shampooing with gasoline, and taking out-of-date aspirin. And this omission is their personal and financial privacy.

So think of this book as flood insurance. If the river near you has not yet started to rise, I can show you how to move to higher ground. If the river is already rising, I hope at least to show you how to build a raft. And just because the river has never flooded before does not mean it will never flood in the future. Unexpected torrential downpours can come in many forms.

PHYSICAL HARM

In Europe, rapes and murders are just a fraction of the number committed in the United States. No nation on earth has more guns per capita, and few if any have a larger percentage of the population in prison. Besides the muggers, the robbers, and the serial killers, you may suddenly be confronted by:

- An irate neighbor, a fellow worker, or a disgruntled client.
- An ex-spouse, an ex-lover, or an ex-employee.
- In-laws, outlaws, or someone mentally deranged.
- A kidnapper, a burglar, or a con man.

MENTAL HARM

The mental damage from worry and fear can be even more devastating than a physical attack. This may come from:

- Stalkers, investigators, or anonymous phone calls in the night.
- Telephone conversations secretly taped, then passed around . . .
- "Confidential" medical records released to your employer, your clients, or your insurance company. These records might divulge mental problems, impotence, abortion, alcohol/drug abuse, a sexual disease, or [fill in the blanks].

FINANCIAL HARM

Make a random list of twenty people you know. On the average, six of them have already been sued, or will be in the future. Lawsuits are not filed only because of accidents, negligence, separations, divorces, or contract disputes. In the United States, anyone can sue anyone else.

One of Wiley Miller's *Non Sequitur* cartoon strips is entitled LEGAL MUGGING. It shows a businessman on the sidewalk of a dark street with his hands in the air. A sign on a post reads "CAUTION: *Watch for trial attorneys.*" Stepping from a narrow alley is a lawyer wearing a stocking cap, dark glasses, and holding out a legal document.

"This is a frivolous lawsuit," says the attorney to his victim. "You can either spend years and thousands of dollars defending yourself, or we can settle out of court right now."

Although this was in a comic strip, what it portrays is not comical. More than one million lawsuits are filed each year in this country. How many of those do you think are frivolous, but are nevertheless settled out of court? Thousands of private investigators would be out of work tomorrow if lawyers stopped employing them to find out who has "deep pockets," that is— who has enough money to make a lawsuit worthwhile.

By putting into practice what you will learn in the pages to follow, you may well be able to shield yourself from lawsuits and the resulting financial harm.

TOTALLY UNFORESEEN TIDAL WAVES

You peek out your window. Look! Reporters, photographers, and trucks with big satellite dishes! If you think this cannot happen to *you*, then kindly allow me to give you a homework assignment. From this day forward, when you read your newspaper or watch the news on TV, start searching for cases where an unknown person is suddenly thrust into the national spotlight. Then ask yourself, *Could this possibly happen to me?*

Here are just a few of the many things that could bring the media, or worse, to your home address:

- A bomb goes off, you were in the area, the FBI thinks you fit the profile . . .
- You win the lottery. (More tears have been shed over winning a lottery than not winning one.)
- An Ident-a-Sketch of the person who robbed the convenience store at 11:45 last night is flashed on TV, and it looks just like you! And you don't have a plausible alibi for that time that anyone's going to believe.
- You were innocently involved with the wrong people and the *60 Minutes* crew has just tracked you down.
- Someone faked your e-mail address when searching for "young virgins" on the Internet and the postal inspectors (yes, the Net is now in their jurisdiction) are about to confiscate your computer.

Do not for a moment think that the information to follow is of mere academic interest—it maybe useful beyond your wildest imagination. A recent article in *Newsweek*, titled "Getting the Wrong Man," gives a chilling example of something that occurs more often than we care to think about.

"Tom Kennedy found the body of his wife, Irene, who had been strangled and stabbed 29 times while on her daily stroll through a park in the Boston suburb of Walpole. Then, a few hours later, the police called at a nearby dilapidated bungalow where Eddie Burke, a 48-year-old handyman, lived with his mother . . . He was practically a textbook match for police profilers: a loner who knew the victim and was clearly eccentric."

[What on earth does "eccentric" mean? My best friends—with a smile—call *me* eccentric. Do I, therefore, fit a certain profile?]

"Burke was visibly nervous and gave contradictory answers when questioned by investigators."

[Wouldn't you be nervous, too?]

"There was blood on his clothes and hands. And forensic dentists would soon match his teeth with bite marks left on Mrs. Kennedy's breast."

Burke was arrested for murder. Within twenty-four hours, the police learned that the DNA from the saliva on Mrs. Kennedy's chest could not have come from Burke. Did they then release him?

"Incredibly, they ran more tests, which again exonerated him. In addition, blood found on Burke turned out to be feline; he had been tending to injured cats. A palm print left on Mrs. Kennedy's thigh didn't match Burke's hand, while the bite-mark evidence proved inconclusive . . . Yet for six weeks, police kept insisting they had the right man in jail . . . While he was locked away, Burke's life was put under a microscope. He was demonized in newspapers and on TV, each story accompanied by a menacing courtroom image of Burke. The sociopathic profiles were fueled by details of his home's contents—X-rated videotapes, kitchen knives, the book *Men Who Hate Women and the Women Who Love Them.* 'They didn't mention the three Bibles in my room,' Burke says. 'They could just as easily said I was a religious fanatic.' "

The police claim they followed a logical course and "had the backing of reputed scientific experts." Let us assume that is correct. The point is that even though Burke was the wrong man, *the contents of his house were published by the media.*

Suppose *you* are suddenly arrested, even though innocent, and the contents of your home are made public? Would anything on the following list—if found in your house—give you cause for concern?

- Excess cash.
- Guns and ammunition.
- Telephone records of all long-distance calls.
- Books, magazines, brochures, correspondence.
- Empty whiskey bottles or evidence of substance abuse.

- Statements from your bank, your broker, your credit-card company.

- The contents on your computer's hard drive, including so-called deleted files, along with a list of sites you once entered on the World Wide Web.

If the police are after you, whether you are guilty or not, what is your first priority? Is it not *time?*

You need time to think, time to get certain items out of the house, time to locate your attorney, or—heaven forbid—time to pick up some cash, arrange transportation, and flee. This book is designed to give you that time, and to help you keep your private information private.

Before we continue, let me say that if someone with *unlimited funds* is after you, you will eventually be found. If you doubt this, contact a competent (repeat: competent) private investigator and say, "I wish to disappear so completely that even you couldn't find me. Can you help me?" The six-word answer will be, "No, because I can find anyone!"

And I agree. Repeatedly, private investigators (PIs) make this point in their books, articles, and personal interviews. And if the police are truly after you, *their* record isn't bad either. Captain Robert L. Snow, a police officer for more than twenty-five years, says in his book *Protecting Your Life, Home, and Property* that the Indianapolis Police Department finds 98 or 99 percent of all persons reported to them as missing.

But in the private investigator section of my home library, I find no PIs anywhere who will admit defeat under any circumstances, *as long as payment is forthcoming.* The closest I can come to a failure is a certain PI who says he successfully tracked down 298 of the 299 targets he was given over his lifetime. As for the one he missed, he eventually concluded that he was given false information, that *no such person ever existed.*

The fuel that runs a private investigator's engine is M-O-N-E-Y. In your present situation, a PI may discover your home address with a single phone call, and come up with a list of your assets the next day. The purpose of this book, then, is to:

1. Plug the immediate loopholes in your security.

2. Put you on guard, before you ever again give out your Social Security number, home address, or correct date of birth, to anyone other than a government agency.

3. Make it so expensive to trace you and/or your assets that the bad guys or gals will give up before achieving their goals.

The direct correlation between money and results cannot be overemphasized. In the sections to come, I'll be referring to various levels of security, with a general outline as follows. However, there may be no clear-cut divisions between one level and the next—it depends on who is after you, why, and the price he or she is willing to pay.

Level One: Very basic, economical moves that will give you more privacy than 98 percent of the general population. Your telephone will be unlisted and your mailing address will not be connected in any way to where you actually live. The opposition might have to pay a private investigator several hundred dollars to track you down.

Level Two: At this point your utilities and your telephone will be in alternate names. The license plates on your vehicles will not reveal your name or true address. Your trash will be shredded. The PI may now charge several thousand dollars to track you down.

Level Three: Welcome to my Level! You and your family have now taken some serious privacy measures. Your home (or rental property) will be in the name of a trust. Each vehicle will be in the name of a limited-liability company. No bank account nor business activity can be traced back to you. When you travel, you will register at motels using an alternate name. The black-hat boys and/or the law firms may have to pay a PI some truly serious money to track you down. Are you worth that much to them? If not, sleep well.

Level Four: At this level you are duplicating the federal Witness Security Program (incorrectly called the Witness "Protection" Program in the media) for criminals protected by the U.S. government. When the Feds do it for a felon, it's legal. When you do it for yourself, it's illegal. Your bridges are now ashes, your friends and relatives just a distant memory. You've canceled all magazine and newsletter subscriptions, cut all ties with clubs, hobbies, and religion, no longer file tax returns, and will never again work for an employer. You may feel this is necessary if there's a bounty on your head or a contract on your life, but at this point, is life still worth living?

If so, keep running, because you can *still* be found. The PI, however, must now have unlimited funds at his disposal, and will call for help. Just as pinned-down soldiers on a battlefield call in air strikes, PIs call in investigative reporters. These are the men who dig up celebrity skeletons for tabloids such as the *National Enquirer*, the *Globe*, and the *Star*. Don't underestimate them. These guys are good—the best in the business.

I recommend you start working on Level One even before you finish reading this book. In the weeks and months to come, raise yourself to Level Two. After that, decide whether or not you wish to ease up to Level Three. It may look difficult at first, but countless others have done it, and so can you. Not only is it easier than you think, but it is fun as well, and leads to a more stress-free life.

However, you must first ask yourself the following question:

WHO SHALL I TRUST?

In 1978, a short, balding man named Stanley Mark Rifkin worked at the Security Pacific National Bank in Los Angeles.

Security Pacific thought of him as a computer programmer but Rifkin thought of himself as a consummate thief.

On October 25 he entered the bank, crossed the lobby, and took the elevator up to the wire transfer room. From this room, hundreds of millions of dollars passed every day from Security Pacific through the Federal Reserve system and on to international banks. Rifkin, identifying himself as the bank's computer consultant, was not challenged as he walked into the heavily guarded room. By interviewing one of the workers, he learned the routing instructions, transfer routines, and the day's security code. Before he left, he memorized an employee access code from an information board on the wall. Later that day, posing as a branch manager, he called the wire room.

"This is Mike Hansen on International."

"Okay, and the office number?" asked a friendly female voice.

"It's 286."

"And the code?"

"Code is 4739."

"Okay."

Now came the moment Rifkin had been living for.

"The bank," he said, speaking in a calm voice, "is Irving Trust in New York City. Payment is to Wozchod Bank, Zurich, Switzerland. The amount is ten million two hundred thousand even."

"Okay, and what's the interoffice settlement number?"

"Let me check. I'll call you right back." He phoned another number at the bank. Pretending to be calling from the wire room, he asked for the settlement number. They gave it to him, and he called the wire room again. The clerk then typed his order into the system. Rifkin had just pulled off one of the largest bank thefts in history. Before the day was out, he was high above the Atlantic, bound for Europe.

In Switzerland, he purchased 250,000 raw diamonds, weighing nearly four pounds. (Raw diamonds are easy to sell and cannot be traced.) At this point it appeared that Rifkin had pulled off the perfect crime. No one at Security Pacific even knew the money was gone! However there are conflicting stories as to what happened next.

Some say he had an ego problem, and couldn't help showing the diamonds to his friends. Others say he bragged about the heist to his lawyer and "trusted friend," assuming he was protected by the attorney-client privilege. Whatever the case, *someone* told the FBI. They chased him, they caught him, and he went to prison.

My original choice for a quote at the beginning of this section was from *Poor Richard's Almanac*. There, Benjamin Franklin wrote, "Three may keep a secret, if two of them are dead." Stanley should have followed Ben's advice.

However, you and I have not stolen any money, nor are we on the run for murder, so there will be few if any instances where if three know our secret, two must be dead. I cite the Rifkin case not out of admiration for his cunning but as an example of stupidity.

Francis Beaumont, one of England's most popular playwrights in the age of Shakespeare, had this to say about secrets: "All confidence which is not absolute and entire is dangerous. There are few occasions but where a man ought either to say all, or conceal all, for, how little ever you have revealed of your secret to a friend, you have already said too much if you think it not safe to make him privy to all particulars."

Allow me to rephrase his comment, boiled down to plain language of the 2000s: *Do not trust your attorney, CPA, private detective, banker, doctor, dentist, school authorities, relatives, family, friends, or anyone else unless you would trust them with your life.*

Here is my own short list of who I do and do not trust:

- *Family:* I trust my wife. I always trusted my parents, but they are dead. I see no reason to confide confidential matters in our grown children, or in their spouses, nor in our grandchildren. I love my millionaire kid sister in Hollywood but do not tell her my secrets. (Sorry, Sis!)

- *Attorneys:* I did trust one in the Canary Islands, but he died before this book went to press. (Another one in said islands took money from my enemies to give me incorrect advice!) I still trust an attorney in San Francisco that I have had on retainer for the past ten years. He has been tested and was not found wanting. Another one in Oakland looks OK as of this writing.

- *CPAs, bankers, doctors, dentists:* One CPA in Texas. None of the others.

- *Private investigators:* Some of my clients are PIs and look to me for advice. There are a few good PIs, a number of mediocre PIs, and a sizable number that are badly bent. To date, I have never had to trust a PI. Should the need come up in the future, I would probably choose one of the PI/authors listed on pages 248–249 because they have reputations too valuable to risk with a betrayal.

PRIVACY

This book has a single theme: *How to keep your private life private.* It is not about avoiding taxes nor specifically about protecting your assets, although the latter is an added benefit. Nor is it a call to disobey the law. I consider myself a law-abiding, tax-paying citizen of the world. Okay, perhaps the way I travel by air is a little odd, and I do confess that I am allergic to certain kinds of permits. However, if I mention any procedure which I suspect might be construed as illegal in some states or provinces, I will warn you of that fact beforehand and let you make your own decision. (Although I've made privacy my business for decades, I'm not a lawyer. So, to repeat, don't take action without the advice and counsel of a trained legal professional.)

For example, you may wish to operate a legitimate but anonymous business from your home. This means you may ignore the requirements for a business license and also the resale tax permit (assuming you live in a sales-tax state). The city will lose a small fee when you don't pay for a license. On the other hand, the state will gain when you pay sales taxes for supplies that might otherwise be exempt. Other small pluses and minuses will enter in. Depending upon the community, there may or may not be any penalty if you are caught, other than catching up on some payment you failed to make. So then, please note:

- My job is to explain the options.
- Your job is to make the decisions.

WHAT MAKES THIS BOOK UNIQUE?

- *Author's qualifications:* My only business is privacy. I live, eat, sleep, and breathe privacy. I have been living a private life since 1959.
- *Anti-offshore:* I do not suggest you leave the country, nor do I recommend foreign corporations, trusts, or bank accounts. You can accomplish your goals right here— cheaper, better, and safer.
- *Lukewarm on corporations:* With few exceptions, I will save you the expense and trouble of forming a corporation, and I will steer you away from Delaware and Nevada.
- *New alternative:* I will recommend a legal entity in a certain state—one that I have never seen discussed in print— that, formed correctly, can never be traced back to you. No managers, no directors, no annual report. *Nada.*
- *No ranting or raving:* Well, maybe a little ranting but definitely no raving about Big Brother, jack-booted government thugs, or the Internal Revenue Service. This is a book about Life in the Real World, not a treatise about the constitution or the Bill of Rights and common law.

- *Up-to-date advice for the year 2001 and beyond:* Any book written prior to this year will be out-of-date when it comes to police powers, e-mail accounts, ChoicePoint, DCS 1000, limited liability companies, commercial mail-receiving agencies, and the increasing danger in giving out your correct date of birth. Although no book can be completely up-to-the-minute, since laws and procedures are constantly changing, I maintain a Web site, www.howtobeinvisible.com, specifically for you readers. Go there for the latest information about personal and business privacy. The password for the update link is ssndob.

HOW TO USE THIS BOOK

Each chapter deals with basic, step-by-step information. Although I explain new terms when they are first introduced, if you run across a word or initials you do not understand, please consult the glossary on page 245. Many of the chapters have a section for questions and answers at the end so if you want more information, do review them. But otherwise, feel free to jump ahead to the next chapter. You may decide to skip some chapters that you feel do not apply to you. However:

Do not skip the next chapter. Your journey to invisibility must begin with the way in which your receive your mail.

QUESTIONS & ANSWERS

Why are you against offshore trusts, when this is recommended by attorneys and promoters at so many seminars?

Despite all the books, Internet advertising, and island-based seminars, I cannot recommend them. (Those that do are, of course, often selling a product.) Many seem to overlook the Small Business Protection Act of 1996. The code provision (IRC Section 6048-c) says a taxpayer who receives a distribution from a foreign trust shall "make a return" which includes the name of the trust, the amount of the distribution, and "such other information as the Secretary [of the Treasury] may prescribe."

When this information is supplied, all hope of secrecy is lost.

What about offshore corporations?

Same answer, even though I once used them myself. Every year the risk of trouble increases, as reporting requirements are amplified and tax-haven governments are subjected to increasing pressure from the United States government. If you fill out the required reports, you compromise your privacy. If you don't fill them out and are caught, you can go to jail.

How about offshore banks?

You mean, to maintain secrecy? If there is one common denominator in all the reports I receive about tax havens, it is about the increasing likelihood of offshore banks being forced by U.S. authorities into revealing confidential information.

I buy all the latest books on privacy and security and I pay out thousands of dollars for magazines and newsletters in this field. Not a month goes by without reading a warning that in such-and-such a tax haven, privacy and secrecy are being whittled away. Why go offshore when you can accomplish similar goals right in the United States?

Are there any hidden dangers in offshore communications?

Yes, and the name of this danger is ECHELON, which is run by the supersecret National Security Agency. The NSA, with its forty thousand employees—including more mathematicians than any other organization in the world!—is the mother of all snooping operations. It monitors all electronic communications that cross national borders, including e-mail, phone calls, faxes, and shortwave radio signals on the airline and maritime frequencies.

German author Rudolph Kippenhahn, in his new book *Code Breaking*, says, "There is some evidence that the NSA also has access to the data flow between world banks."

An article in the May 31, 1999, *Business Week* had this to say about the NSA's Echelon: "Americans should know that every time they place an international call, the NSA is listening," says John E. Pike, a military analyst at the Federation of American Scientists in Washington. "Just get used to the fact—Big Brother is listening."

What Big Brother listens or watches for are key words, including all known slang words for drugs, cash, smuggling, bombs, etc. Therefore, *avoid all such words*.

Example: One of my American clients is arranging for untraceable hawala exchanges (see Chapter 14) between California and Madrid. He first mailed a list of substitute words to his contact in Madrid, so that they can continue to use e-mail. However, it will appear they are discussing another subject, where words like "dollars," "pesetas," "exchange rate," and "bank" will NOT be used.

What is "Carnivore"?

The name Carnivore has been changed to DCS1000. It's a specialized software installed by the FBI on an Internet service provider's network under federal wiretap authority. It is capable of keeping tabs on your e-mail, instant messages, and Web-surfing activities. The system is ripe for abuse because of the secrecy surrounding how it scans passing data to find its targets. One likely way to circumvent both Echelon and DCS1000 would be to create and save your entire message as a picture and simply send it along with a message like, "Picture of the new baby." (This is called steganography and is discussed in chapter 17.)

2

U.S. MAIL—SENDING IT, RECEIVING IT

Do not, as long as you live, ever again allow your real name to be coupled with your home address.

—J. J. Luna

Washington state resident Elizabeth Reed, 28, dated Anthony Nitsch, Jr., 32, for about two months in the fall of 1996. Then, concerned about his drinking, Elizabeth told Anthony the relationship was over. When she stopped taking his calls, he became angry and began stalking and harassing her.

She continued to live at the same address.

Anonymous packages arrived at her home, one with a dead skunk, another with a sex toy and an obscene message. Strange items began to appear in her yard. Someone disconnected her heat-pump fuse box and defecated on it. Her fiancé came to visit her, and when he returned to his car he discovered the tires had been slashed.

Two years passed. Elizabeth Reed continued to live at the same address. She went to a judge and sought a restraining order against Anthony Nitsch, Jr. The judge refused to grant it because

Elizabeth could not prove Anthony was the person who was harassing her.

On a warm Monday night in early June, Anthony cut the telephone line that led into her home. Then he broke in, threatened her, and fired one shot at her from a .40 handgun.

The ending of this story is not as sad as might normally be the case. I have before me the *Tacoma News Tribune* dated June 5, 1998. The headline on page three reads, "Intruder who was shot held for $500,000 bail." Although Elizabeth Reed had failed to move away, she was armed and ready. Nitsch missed. She did not. "Nitsch remained in serious condition Wednesday," says the article, "at Harborview Medical Center with five gunshot wounds to his chest."

TO MOVE OR NOT TO MOVE

Mexican journalist Fernando Balderas and his wife Yolanda Figueroa wrote a book called *The Boss of the Gulf: The Life and Capture of Juan Garcia Abrego*, which was published in August 1996. The book was dedicated to Mexico's federal attorney general, Antonio Lozano Gracia. At that time Fernando and Yolanda lived, with their children Patricia, Paul, and Fernando, in an attractive home in an upscale neighborhood in Mexico City. Although nothing in the book appeared to warrant retribution, it did discuss Mexico's drug lords and revealed bribery in high circles. What follows is from the December 9, 1996, edition of *USA Today*:

> MEXICO CITY—Police found journalist Fernando Balderas, his author wife, Yolanda Figueroa, and their three children, ages 18, 13, and 8, bludgeoned to death in their beds last week . . . a brutal murder that shocked even hardened residents. Adding to the intrigue: Police say the family was probably murdered Tuesday night, a day after President Ernesto Zedillo fired Mexico's federal attorney

general Antonio Lozano Gracia, to whom the Figueroa's
book was dedicated.

When President Zedillo fired the guy their book was dedicated
to, they should have fled their home that very day. (Reason:
Guilt by association—especially applicable among drug lords and
crooked politicians.) Some say that if the bad guys are out to get
you, there's nothing you can do, but I disagree. You can be seen
in public but still keep your home address *private*.

I suspect that the Balderas family did indeed think about moving, but then decided it would be too much trouble. Trust me
on this one: Trouble or not, moving is better. However, even if
all is quiet and you are unable or unwilling to move at this time,
I urge you to take the recommended steps in this and succeeding
chapters. As you will see, there are legitimate ways to disconnect
your name from your property, your telephone, your utilities,
your licenses, and yes—even on your tax returns and your
driver's license. The place to start is with home deliveries, be
that by mail, by UPS, by FedEx or by your local pizza parlor.

If you plan to move within the year, perhaps you will stall on
some of the other suggestions. Do not, however, delay on this
one. If there is only one lesson you carry away from this book,
let it be the one listed at the beginning of this chapter:

*Do not, as long as you live, ever again allow your real name to
be coupled with your home address.*

If you are still not convinced, consider the case of George
Joseph Cvek, as presented in the book *Diary of a D.A.* by Martin
M. Frank, formerly an assistant district attorney in the Bronx. I
quote from page 168:

Included is number 1314 Virginia Avenue, where, at about 2:45
on the afternoon of January 13th, the doorbell of an apartment
rang. That ring set off one of the greatest manhunts in the history
of the New York Police Department. Although it was like the
sound of countless other doorbells, in the succeeding months it
was to echo and re-echo from Maine to Louisiana and beyond

the Mississippi to Nebraska. It was the signal for a chase where the quarry was an unknown, unnamed individual whose description might fit millions of men in that vast area.

When the doorbell rang on that January afternoon, a young housewife opened her apartment door to find a slim, ordinary looking man of about twenty-eight standing at the threshold. He was a stranger to her.

"Are you Mrs. Allen?" he asked.

"Yes, I am."

"Is your husband home?"

"No," she replied, "he isn't here now."

"Gee, I'm sorry," he said. "I know him from Norwalk, Connecticut. I thought this was his early day. Maybe I'll come back tonight." He seemed rather well acquainted with her husband, a route salesman in Connecticut for a bakery company.

The caller half turned to go, then stopped and apologetically asked, "Could I have a drink of water?"

"Sure," she said, "wait here a second." Leaving him at the door, Mrs. Allen went into the kitchen. When she returned, she found that he had walked through the foyer into the living room and was seated on the sofa. . . .

The caller continued to deceive Mrs. Allen, then suddenly struck her down and prepared to rape her. At that moment, the telephone rang. He jumped up and ran from the apartment, slamming the door behind him. But in the years to come, more than two hundred women were not so fortunate. Their telephones did not ring. In virtually every case, the caller gained entrance by telling the wife he knew her husband, and after gaining entrance through subterfuge, he raped and killed her, then burglarized the home. In each case it was the husband himself who had unwittingly given the villain—who was eventually identified as George Joseph Cvek—information about himself and, when asked for an address so Cvek could mail him a small gift, gave him his *home address*. At that instant *he sealed his wife's death warrant.*

This is but one of many chilling examples of allowing mail to come to your home address. In fact, there are dangers not only in receiving mail but in sending it out, as we shall see.

MAIL THEFT

Every day more than one hundred thousand residential mailboxes in the United States are burglarized. This applies to mail being received both in the city and in the country, both in private homes and in apartment complexes. In Hammond, Indiana, before they were finally arrested, two men and a woman went from door to door but did not knock or ring any bells. The neighbors saw nothing more suspicious than each person depositing an advertising brochure in each mailbox. What they didn't see was the sleight of hand when the person traded the brochure for whatever mail was in the box.

The *Seattle Post–Intelligencer* recently ran an article warning of mail theft not only from home mailboxes but from mail collection boxes on the street, plus the boxes used at thousands of apartments, condominiums, and commercial buildings in the Northwest. It seems that for months, thieves had been using counterfeit "arrow keys." Each arrow key provides access to about 2,500 mail collection boxes, more than 10,000 apartments and condominiums, and virtually all office and commercial buildings in the region. (The keys give postal workers easy access to the mailboxes, making it easier for them to pick up and deliver messages and packages.)

Readers were urged to stop using outside mailboxes to deposit mail, including their own home mailboxes. Instead, they were to deposit mail only inside a post office.

In addition to professional thieves, it was said that many others have been stealing mail: drug addicts, to support their habit; teenagers, looking for cash; petty thieves, looking for any number of things.

In the article, headlined "THEFT OF MAIL A PROBLEM AT OUR DOORSTEP," U.S. Postal Inspector Jim Bordenet voiced mail security concerns.

"Thieves rifle outgoing mail for checks written to pay bills. They then alter the checks so they can cash them for large amounts. He suggests people not put outgoing mail into their own boxes, and especially advises against using the red flag, which is a signal to thieves.

Thieves sometimes follow carriers around and steal incoming mail, he said. They're typically looking for boxes of checks and credit-card offers."

I will spare you the flurry of follow-up articles and letters to the editor that followed publication of the article just quoted. Some of the questions raised were:

- Why didn't the Postal Service warn the public about such thefts years ago?
- Why was nothing said until the thefts were exposed by the local newspapers?
- Why—even now—is the problem not being solved?

Another article, this one from the McClatchy Newspapers, is datelined Sacramento, March 5, and titled "Post Office Fights Mailbox Theft."

It reports that hundreds of pieces of mail are stolen *daily* in the Sacramento area. In rural areas the criminals watch for raised red flags, the signal that outgoing mail is inside. Others pry open "cluster boxes" at apartment complexes or housing developments and steal everybody's mail at the same time. In some cases they even pry open the standard blue U.S. mail collection boxes. The article quotes Tom Hall, a postal inspector who investigates mail theft from Sacramento to the Oregon border: "Today, thanks to chemicals and computers, thieves can use almost any kind of financial information to commit a variety of financial crimes. If you write a check to a utility and a bad guy gets it, he can 'wash' the utility's name off and make the check out to himself in a higher amount. With that one check, he can also make himself a whole new set of checks under your name." Even worse; continues the article, "some criminals 'assume' the victim's identity and apply for credit cards in the victim's name."

My advice, then, is to *usually* deposit all outgoing mail inside a building. I say "usually" because on March 6, 2001, Juanita Yvette Lozano was indicted by a grand jury in Austin, Texas. (It as alleged that she was the one that mailed a video of George W. Bush's confidential debate-prep material to an Al Gore advisor.) Ms. Lozano's problem was that the Austin, Texas post office has a surveillance camera that takes a video of everyone mailing packages and letters inside the post office. So what does this mean?

Just this: You may be mailing a letter to order a subscription to *Family Circle* magazine, but what if someone else mails a letter about the same time that is considered to be a criminal offense? The next time you are in your local post office, glance around. If you spot a camera, you may wish to find a different place to mail your letters and packages in the future—perhaps a smaller post office or a pickup station inside another business, such as in a strip mall or a supermarket.

By putting these suggestions into practice, what have you accomplished? First of all, you have protected both your incoming and your outgoing mail from random theft. Second, if you have been targeted for any reason, an investigator might be illegally "borrowing" the mail from your home mailbox, reading it, and returning it the next day, apparently unopened. But if no mail comes to your home, he will have nothing to read.

RECEIVING MAIL AT YOUR PRESENT HOME ADDRESS

If you are presently receiving mail at home, you can stop this immediately by turning in a forwarding address. But where should this mail go? Not to any address you will use in the future—once you have sent out the changes of address, the mail will trickle down and then you will close the new temporary address. Here are some options:

1. If you presently have a PO box that can be traced back to you, choose that address. When the forwarding comes to a close, close the PO box.

2. If you still receive mail at a commercial mail-receiving agency ("mail drop"), forward the mail there temporarily. As you will see, the mail drop should be closed down fairly soon.

3. Have it sent on to your place of business if you have one, or perhaps to a friend who is in business.

4. Forward to a friend or relative, preferably across the country. Tell him or her to keep the magazines, toss out the junk mail, and to remail the rest back to you at your *new address*. (You haven't got one yet but be patient. It's coming, it's coming. . . .)

How to forward your mail: With the exception listed below, I suggest you not check the little box marked "Permanent." If you do, your name will go into the Postal Service's National Change of Address list and this list of persons that have moved is sold to the commercial mail-list folks and thus your name and new address will go into countless computers.

Instead, check the "Temporary" box and give a date when this is to end. At the same time, notify the post office that you are moving away and do not wish to have any mail forwarded. Mail will then be returned to sender.

Exception: If you wish to throw others far off the trail, then do file a Permanent Change of Address. I suggest the actual street address of a mail drop in northern Alaska or—if you already live up there—a mail drop in Florida or Hawaii. Here is an easy way to do it:

1. If you have access to the Internet, go to www.mbe.com, the home page of Mail Boxes Etc., or to www.postnet.net, the home page of PostNet. Look up the location you want. Or, look up one of their locations in the phone book, call them, and ask them to give you the address at such-and-such a location.

2. On your forwarding address card, fill out your name, the street address, an apartment number, city, state, and ZIP. Example: Your name is Jane Winner and you want your ex to think you moved to Florida.

If the address you pull up on the Internet is:

MBE #0955
9970 E Osceola Pkwy
Kissimmee, FL 34743

Forward your mail to:

Jane Winner
9970 E Osceola Pkwy
Kissimmee, FL 34743

Here, then, is what will happen. Your mail will be forwarded to the address shown, but because this is a commercial mail receiving agency (CMRA), and no "#" sign followed by a number is included, the envelope will be stamped with a message similar to the one below and will then be returned to the sender.

UNDELIVERABLE, COMMERCIAL
MAIL RECEIVING AGENCY, NO
AUTHORIZATION TO RECEIVE
MAIL FOR THIS ADDRESSEE

Will your local post office, the one forwarding the mail to Florida, know what is happening? No, because the mail does not come back to them.

Will the person you are trying to avoid realize you didn't go there after all? Not necessarily. The stamp on the envelope does not say "No Such Person." It merely says the CMRA not currently accepting mail for you.

RECEIVING MAIL AT YOUR FUTURE HOME ADDRESS

Although we ourselves never receive mail at a home address, two of my clients currently receive *nonpersonal* mail at home for specific reasons:

Rolland moved to a rural area in the summer of 1999. His new address for receiving personal mail is at the home of a widow in the nearest small town, seventeen miles away from where he actually lives. She rents several rooms in her large home. Rolland, however, is a voracious reader and subscribes to more than thirty weekly and monthly magazines. Rather than burden the widow with this volume, he orders each new subscription in what appears to be a business name, R & R Services, and has them come to his rural mailbox at his actual address. He never uses "R & R" for any other purpose whatsoever. Therefore, if his name is run through a national database of magazine subscribers, there will be no trace back to him.

Janet is a single mother with a six-month-old baby. She recently fled from Washington, D.C., to a southern state to escape an ex-lover who was threatening to kill her. She is establishing herself at the new location under another name. She has a new (alternative) address at which she receives mail from her mother and sister, as well as bank statements, telephone bills, and other personal mail. However, she *wants* to make her new name known so she receives *Family Circle* and *Reader's Digest*, as well as small shipments of mail-order vitamins, at her home. The orders and the subscriptions have automatically put her new name into various databases, and she receives Sweepstakes offers and other junk mail in the new name.

"If someone wishes to look at *this* mail," she says, "or even steal it, be my guest!"

THE LATEST PROBLEM WITH CMRAS

You may never have heard of ChoicePoint, but ChoicePoint has almost certainly heard of you. This Alpharetta, Georgia company specializes in doing what the law discourages the government from doing on its own—culling, sorting, and packaging data on individuals from scores of sources, including credit bureaus, marketers, regulatory agencies, and private mailboxes.

The FBI's Investigative Information Services unit, which helps agents obtain information on individuals for their investigations, relies heavily on ChoicePoint's services. On the Web, FBI agents also can go to www.cpfbi.com—'ChoicePoint Online for the FBI'—for help in conducting their own searches. On that Web page, the company's logo appears alongside the FBI's official seal.

ChoicePoint says it buys its primary information for the data products it markets to the government, private detectives, and the media from the nation's three major credit bureaus. They are Equifax Credit Information Services Inc., a unit of former ChoicePoint parent Equifax Inc.; Trans Union LLC and Experian Information Solutions, Inc. Each of the three companies maintains credit histories on more than 180 million Americans.

The company takes these credit-bureau files and retains the portion that lists the consumer's name, known aliases, birthdate, Social Security number, current and prior addresses and phone number. The credit bureaus are valuable sources of such data because their records tend to be up-to-date. That's because people typically tell their creditors when they move, even if they fail to tell the Postal Service.

ChoicePoint indexes this data under the subject's Social Security number and stirs in more information it gleans from other sources. These sources, including local, state, and federal agencies, sell the company data ranging from motor-vehicle, driver and boat registrations, liens and deed transfers to phone listings, military personnel records and voter rolls. By mixing and matching its databases, ChoicePoint can accumulate all kinds of information—a speeding fine, a bankruptcy filing, a spouse's name—under a single Social Security number, tailoring the data and related software to a particular client.

The product lets it check health-care provider's addresses against two million of what ChoicePoint calls "high-risk and fraudulent business addresses."

This includes private mailboxes.

The U.S. Marshals Service has a $3.8 million contract with ChoicePoint and can put out an "alert." If you are the target, the moment you rent a private mailbox at a commercial mail receiving agency *in any state*, they will be notified.

YOUR GHOST ADDRESS

I have been referring to your "new" or "alternate" address but from this point forward it will be called your *ghost* address. A ghost address is one that has no connection with your actual place of residence. How this address is obtained will be explained in the following chapter.

Because the secure sending and receiving of mail has become so complicated, the question-and-answer section that follows is the largest in this book. If you are in a hurry, however, jump to the next chapter. You can always come back here later.

QUESTIONS & ANSWERS

What is a "mail cover?"

This is a system used by a number of governments to check your mail without a court order. Your mailman, or the clerk that "boxes" your mail will be instructed to note the return addresses and country of origin of your incoming mail. If you live a squeaky-clean life, you may say to yourself, imitating *Mad Magazine's* Alfred E. Neuman, "What? Me worry?" Read on:

Suppose you send mail *to* a person or company that is the subject of a mail cover? If you list your name and return address, you yourself could end up on a suspect list. There are at least two obvious solutions:

1. Copy the British—eliminate a return address. Or,

2. Use some other return address, far, far away.

Recently, the postal authorities have been getting more cautious. For any parcel that weighs sixteen ounces or more, the sender must show up in person, and the item must bear a return address. The day may not be far off when a return address will be required for *all* outgoing mail.

I send out large volumes of mail so I use a postage meter. Any danger there?

I don't know how large a volume you refer to, but my wife and I used to mail up to two thousand letters a week on a regular basis. We had a regular system, using thirty-three-cent self-adhesive stamps. First, we stuck one stamp on each finger, then we put them on four envelopes, one, two, three, four, and repeat.

Why didn't we use a postage meter? Because each postage meter has an identification number that ties it to a renter and to a specific location, that's why.

Does it matter if—unsure of the exact postage—I put on more than enough stamps?

Judge for yourself: I know of a case in Missouri where a man put $38 postage on a small package that weighed less than two pounds. Destination, Los Angeles, but it didn't arrive. In view of the excess postage, the Drug Enforcement Administration (DEA) was called in and the package turned out to contain $10,000 in cash. Although I do not know if the source of the money was legal, privacy newsletters claim that the DEA "arrests" and keeps most confiscated cash, even though the owner may never be convicted of anything. Actually, cash can be mailed most anywhere using many envelopes and small sums per envelope. With $38 the Missourian could have bought 118 first-class stamps. Had he then put just three one-hundred-dollar bills in each envelope, wrapping the money with a page or two from a magazine, he could have mailed out, not $10,000, but $35,000. And if mailed on different days from various post offices, and with a variety of fictitious return addresses, would anyone even have a clue?

This was not the first time I heard of incorrect postage alerting the authorities. One of the telltale signs postal inspectors look for, in the case of letter bombs, is "excess postage." I use an electronic scale that measures in both pounds and grams and I double-check all outgoing mail.

At present, I receive a daily newspaper in my own name. It goes into its own box alongside my rural mailbox. Is there some way to at least continue to receive my daily paper, both at my present home, and at the new one when I move?

At one time we had a Canadian newspaper delivered directly to a holiday home under another name. No longer. Too many cases like the one cited in Carson City's *Nevada Appeal*, headed, "Minden teen appears in court, may face 15 charges." The charges were that three teenagers burglarized houses in the Carson Valley *while the occupants were away*. And how did they know the occupants were away? From "information allegedly obtained through his job as a newspaper carrier." Nevertheless, if you cannot live without your daily newspaper(s), then at least heed this advice:

- Cancel the newspaper that you now receive. A month later, order a new subscription under another name. Avoid paying the newspaper carrier in person.
- When you leave on a trip, do not have the newspapers held. Get a friend or neighbor to pick them up. (Nevertheless, the best way is still to have the newspaper delivered to your ghost address.)

How secure is my incoming mail?

That depends on where it's coming from, what it looks like, and who your enemies are. Under normal circumstances I have far more confidence in regular mail (often referred to as snail mail) than in electronic mail, because there is no possible way to scan the interiors of *all* the millions of letters in the U.S. postal system at any one time. Contrast this with electronic mail, which can be computer-searched at every junction along the way, red-flagging messages with any of hundreds or thousands of key words such as bomb, gas, gun, rifle, money, cash, or with any specific name including yours.

Note, however, that certain government officials *do* monitor mail from tax-haven countries, especially those on the following list:

Andorra, Antigua, Aruba, Austria, the Bahamas, Belize, Bermuda, British Virgin Islands, Cayman Islands, Channel Islands, Colombia, Cook Islands, Gibraltar, Guernsey, Isle of Man, Liberia, Liechtenstein, Luxembourg, Marshall Islands, Nauru, Nevis, Panama, Turks and Caicos Islands, and Vanuatu.

Also, what do your incoming letters look like? If you are in my age bracket, you may remember when your mother dripped hot red wax on the flap of an envelope, then pressed a seal into the wax before it cooled. The more modern method is to seal the flaps with clear tape. Neither is secure, and both methods (especially the red wax seal!) draw unwanted attention to the envelope, saying "Something valuable in here."

Further, anyone with a spray can of freon gas—sold under various trade names in spy shops—can read what's inside without opening the envelope at all. When hit with the spray, the envelope becomes transparent. Thirty seconds later, as the gas evaporates, it returns to its normal condition, with no evidence of this intrusion. (The defense against this is to ask the sender to address the envelope by hand with a felt-tip pen, or with a fountain pen that uses regular ink. The ink will run when the freon is sprayed on the envelope, thus at least tipping you off that the mail was read.)

Methods once confined to the CIA are now common knowledge, thanks (?) to Paladin Press. They publish the CIA *Flaps and Seals Manual* that carefully details "surreptitious entries of highly protected items of mail." Using carbon tetrachloride to remove transparent tape from an envelope is at the elementary level. What worries the CIA and other surreptitious readers of secret mail is not the sealed or taped envelope but the normal one.

"The most innocuous-looking envelope," says the CIA manual, "may be the one that will get the operator in the most trouble." Right! So let's talk about innocuous-looking envelopes next.

Protecting letters you mail out. Remember, the envelope should appear normal. A junk-mail appearance is best (make sure the one receiving it *knows* that!) and for that reason I prefer a standard #10 envelope with a laser-printed label. If a sealed, taped, or otherwise obviously protected envelope is desired, enclose and protect everything in a #9 envelope and insert that one in the #10 envelope. If you are not familiar with envelope numbers, note these measurements:

#10 envelope:	$4\frac{1}{8} \times 9\frac{1}{2}$ inches
#9 envelope:	$3\frac{7}{8} \times 8\frac{7}{8}$ inches

To counteract the envelope's transparency when sprayed with freon, wrap the contents of the #9 envelope with carbon paper, if you can still find it in this modern age.

Remailing letters from other cities in the United States: From time to time, you may wish to have it appear that you are in a certain area. I do not say "city," since huge areas are now included in a postmark from such cities as Denver, Dallas, and Detroit. Here is the easiest way:

Prepare your letter, seal it in an addressed #9 envelope (available at any office-supply store), and put on the correct postage. Enclose your letter in a #10 envelope, add a cover letter as shown below, and a $5 bill. Note that you don't use a last name, so there is no way to prove you were not a guest.

> *Sheraton El Conquistador*
> *Attention: Concierge*
> *I was a recent guest at your hotel, and most impressed with your fine service. I do, however, have a small problem, and I must ask you a favor.*
> *During my Arizona stay, I promised to write to an associate while in Tucson. I forgot to do this, so would you kindly help me cover my derrière by mailing the enclosed letter?*
> *I include $5 for your trouble, and hope to thank you in person when I return to the Sheraton El Conquistador later this year.*
> *Yours sincerely,*
> *Jim*

Mail your letter to "Concierge" at one of the very best hotels in the city of your choice. (You can get the name and address from AAA, or off the Internet.) Here is a sample of how to address the envelope:

> *For the CONCIERGE:*
> Sheraton El Conquistador
> 10000 North Oracle Road
> Tucson, Arizona 85737

Note: If there is some doubt that the hotel has a concierge, just address the letter to "Reception." (If there isn't a reception desk, you've chosen too small a hotel.)

From now on, when you travel, pick up sample envelopes and letterheads from luxury hotels. Staying at them is best, but you can often drift up to the desk when they're busy with check-ins and kindly ask for "a sheet of paper and an envelope." One of each is enough, as you'll never use a specific hotel for re-mailing more than *once.*

Remailing letters from anywhere in Europe: The procedure is sim-ilar to remailing from the U.S. but with two exceptions.

First, you must ask the concierge to put on correct postage for overseas airmail, so I suggest you enclose at least $7 or $8, preferably $10. The ideal way to do this is to enclose the local currency, but if not available, then U.S. bills will serve.

Tip: When you hear of a friend who's going to Europe, have him or her bring you postage stamps for overseas airmail, and local currency equivalents of $5 to $10 from as many countries as possible. And if this is a *really* good friend, ask for letterheads and envelopes from various hotels, picture postcards, a pad of typing paper, and a pack of size DL envelopes from an office-supply store. You never know when this foresight might prove to be most opportune!

Second, European envelopes and stationery are not the same size as in the United States and Canada, so using 8½ × 11 inch paper and a #10 envelope may be a giveaway. Here are the Eur-opean sizes:

A4 paper	210 × 297 mm	(about 8¼ × 12 inches)
DL envelopes	110 × 220 mm	(about 4⅜ × 8¾ inches)
Personal envelopes	120 × 176 mm	(4¾ × 7 inches)

You can fake the size A4 paper. Just buy legal size 11½ × 14 inch paper and cut it with a paper cutter (*not* by hand) to 8½ × 12 inches. Or, if you're into European remailing big-time, have a print shop cut sheets to these specifications. The envelopes you'll have to order.

If you write to a law firm, trust company, or bank—especially overseas—it might be better not to identify the office or institution in the address. Instead, use an individual name, someone that works there. If you don't know any of the names, address the letter to "Office Manager" or "Secretary," avoiding any mention of a bank, law office, or trust company.

3

YOUR "GHOST" ADDRESS

. . . a verbal phantom, a shadow of a shade.
—ZOUCH: LIFE OF WALTON

More than half the people who come to me for help, wishing to keep various assets invisible to others, *see no problem in having their home address known.* Yes, some may be able to get by, but for others with this kind of attitude, it can be a matter of life and death.

An extreme viewpoint? Mike Ketcher of Burnsville, Minnesota, editor of *The Financial Privacy Report*, certainly doesn't think so. He hired Yon Soon Yoon, a divorced woman, to work in his office. Yon Soon's ex-husband, Jae Choe, had been harassing her for years. When Mike hired Yon Soon, Choe was furious. Eventually he went on a rampage, shooting Yon Soon, their fourteen-year-old son, John, and two policemen, after which he killed himself. The publisher of the newsletter, Daniel Rosenthal, sums up the two important lessons learned, as follows:

FIRST, if you think the police are there to protect you, let me tell you differently. Yon Soon had a restraining order against Choe. So did we, at our home and our office. But the police ignored our repeated requests to enforce these restraining orders, despite Choe's continual violations and threats. On several occasions they literally laughed at our requests for enforcement.

SECOND, when the police don't work, privacy DOES work. The only person in our company that was truly safe was Mike Ketcher. He was safe because he kept his personal affairs so private that Mr. Choe couldn't find him.

Let me repeat that last part once more: Mike Ketcher was safe because he kept his personal affairs *so private* that Mr. Choe couldn't find him.

In the context of this book, a ghost address refers to a future address you will use that has no connection to where you really live. Although I will usually speak of this address in the singular, you may wish to have multiple ghost addresses. In my own case, I use one address for my clients, a second address for bank statements, utilities, and telephone bills, and a third address for my tax returns. For my driver's license in a faraway state I use a fourth address. I have a fifth address for the companies that own my cars and my boat, and my sixth address is a CMRA address in Canada, where commercial mail-receiving agencies are still private. These are in addition to my two permanent addresses on Spain's Fuerteventura Island. (If you ever happen to vacation in the Canary Islands, don't bother trying to track me down in "Morro Jable, LP de GC." You could grow old and die before you succeed. . . .)

A PARTIAL LIST WHERE YOUR GHOST ADDRESS(ES) WILL BE USED

1. All incoming mail, including from your mother or your children.

2. The Internal Revenue Service.

3. Your driver's license.

4. Any real estate you own.

5. Any loans you have made to others.

6. All licenses for your pets. (A PIs favorite!)

7. Hunting and fishing licenses.

8. Your library card.

9. Your voter's registration. (Some prefer not to vote.)

10. All insurance policies.

11. All utilities: garbage pickup, electric, gas, water.

12. Any membership records, as with your church.

13. Your doctor, dentist, and chiropractor.

14. Your attorney and your accountant.

15. Your pilot's license and airplane registration.

16. All LLCs (see Chapter 12) use to title your vehicles, etc.

17. All purchases, especially where a guarantee is involved.

18. Social Security and Medicare.

19. Rental: home, storage unit, car, tools or whatever.

20. Cable TV. (Another PI favorite!) Be sure the service is not in your name, and that monthly bills go to your ghost address.

Until recently, one small step toward privacy was to rent an address at a commercial mail-receiving agency such as PakMail, PostNet, or Mail Boxes Etc. However, that has now changed.

COMMERCIAL MAIL–RECEIVING AGENCIES (CMRAs), a.k.a. MAIL DROPS

In the spring of 1999, a small news item from the Associated Press was printed on the inside pages of newspapers from coast to coast and sent chills into the hearts of more than a million readers. Under new postal regulations intended to stamp out mail fraud, anonymity was about to disappear for anyone who was renting—or would rent in the future—a private mailbox from places like PostNet and Mail Boxes Etc. From this time onward, not only would government-issued picture ID be required (kept on file) but a special identifier, called a PMB number, would have to be included in the address. This, of course, would tip off stalkers, ex-partners, and freaks and geeks of all persuasions that the addressee was using an alternate address. The following year, the USPS eliminated the PMB requirement if a pound sign preceded the mail box number. However, "suite" "apartment" are still prohibited.

I quickly obtained and read the official thirteen-page government edict. For all practical purposes, it was no longer possible to use these private mailbox services to protect your privacy. Therefore, I sent the following letter to more than one hundred of my clients that were using a certain address. [Names have been changed.]

As you know, my mail-receiving address until now has been Martin & Martin, 500 N. Columbia Road, Suite 20, Grand Forks, ND 58201. The "Martin" refers to my attorney in another state and the mail was of course sent on to an undisclosed location. The N. Columbia Road address was a telephone answering service run from the same location for the past eighteen years by a tough old lady named Maggy. As a sideline, she had 30 mailboxes, mostly for illegal aliens that work on farms in the area. She thought that since she was so small, she would slip through the cracks, but no such luck. Rather than cooperate with what she calls the Postal Service's "Gestapo tactics," she is closing down her mail service. All mail received on or after August 23 will be returned to sender—not by Maggy but by the Grand Forks Post Office.

When I heard this news, I flew to Winnipeg, rented a car, and made a quick trip down to Grand Forks to wind up my affairs with Maggy and to arrange for a new mail drop. I am going to describe what I did in the hope that this may give you some ideas as well. The first step was to make a mental list of small businesses that receive mail for at least several different persons. This included but was not limited to accountants, attorneys, clinics (medical, chiropractic, etc.), real-estate offices, used-car dealers, barbershops, bookstores, coffee shops, bars, contractors, martial-arts studios, tax consultants, RV parks, day-care centers, and mom-and-pop motels.

The next step was to start driving around to look for such businesses. In less than half a mile I came across a real-estate office with three little cabins in the rear. Two of them appeared to be lived in, but the third one was obviously used for storage.

Bingo!

I introduced myself to Jim, the owner. I explained my circumstances and referred him to Maggy at the mail drop. I also offered to have him call my attorney in California if he needed a further reference. (He did not check with either person.)

"I have the perfect setup," he said with a smile. "Cabin 340 back there is just for storage, but it has its own mailbox. C'mon back, I'll show you." Unseen from the main street was a row of rural mailboxes lined up on a wooden crossbar. All were small, old, bent, and dirty. "I get mail here," he said,

*pointing to one of the boxes, "for all seventeen of my sales-
men!" I said he probably needed a larger box, and he said he
certainly did. . . .*

*Bottom line: I said I would put up new, larger mailboxes
for both us, and what could I do for him besides that? Jim
was fascinated about my work as a privacy consultant and
expressed concern about all the things that he owned in his
own name. I am now his consultant and will help him make
some needed changes. I hope the above account has given you
some ideas of your own. My new business address is as shown
below, and all mail should be addressed exactly that way.*
Do not use my name when you address the envelope.

R, M & S
[street address, no suite number]
Grand Forks, ND 58201

In the months that followed, address changes came pouring
in. No one had any questions about how to find a new address.
Apparently the foregoing example was sufficient.

There is a reason for the use of three letters on the top line
of the new (ghost) address. If—heaven forbid!—someone should
send me a letter by registered mail, the person chosen to show
up at the post office will be one of three persons I know in Grand
Forks. Their last names start with R, M, or S. If they have to
show ID, they will identify themselves as one of the three associates in the address. The three-initial address has been working well ever since, with no problems. I highly recommend this
system for at least one of your ghost addresses.

MORE IDEAS FOR OBTAINING GHOST ADDRESSES

Check the yellow pages for small offices that offer business services. Some of the categories might be Accountants, Advertising,
Bookkeeping, Consulting, Insurance, Delivery Services, Office &

Desk Space Rental, and Delivery Services. Don't call them, go
in person. Discuss whatever services they offer, and then, as
you're leaving, imitate Peter Falk in the old *Columbo* shows:

"Oh, *by the way*, do you happen to accept mail here for any
of your clients?" If they do not, move on. If, however, they say,
"Well, only for three or four . . ." see if they will take you on. If
they agree, you can almost certainly be added to their list without showing ID. These small services sort mail by name alone,
without a box number added. The ideal address is one on a street
that also has private residences—the type of street address you
will need for such things as a library card or a driver's license.

An out-of-state address is Level Three privacy at its best. For
this, you will need the help of someone you trust. When your
friend receives mail for you at his home or business address, he
will mail it on to you in a plain envelope. Such an address will
be a necessity if you obtain an out-of-state driver's license because you will need an address in that same state.

Even if you are not yet prepared to use an out-of-state address, keep it in mind for the future. It works best if you know
a certain area well in another state—perhaps because you used
to live there, or visit relatives there. (More will be said about
this in Chapters 12 and 13.)

SHOULD YOU ALLOW ANYONE AT YOUR GHOST ADDRESS TO KNOW WHERE YOU LIVE?

Only you yourself can answer. Hopefully, when you made the
arrangements, you gave an address other than your own, and no
telephone number. However, have they gotten to know you? Do
they recognize your car? If so, might they have seen it in front
of your home? What follows is a chilling example of what unfortunately goes on every day, not only at commercial mail drops
but even at some of the ghost addresses.

Let's call her Sally Overstreet. She is a newspaper reporter who has twice moved to avoid an ex-lover who has been stalking her for years. Unknown to Sally, her stalker is now working with a private investigator, a.k.a. a gumshoe or private eye.

The PI shows up at her ghost address. He is wearing a UPS uniform and carries a box addressed to Sally Overstreet. The return address is that of a major New York publisher. The "UPS" man says he must pick up a certified check for $200 before leaving the box. The next day is a Saturday—or a holiday—and the UPS man insists the box is something Ms. Overstreet has to have TODAY. Could the folks at the ghost address kindly tell him where Ms. Overstreet can be reached? How about a telephone number? Where does she work, maybe the box can be delivered there? This ruse often works, which is why it remains so popular.

The PI in the uniform need not appear to be from the UPS. Perhaps he is from FedEx, Brink's Security, or Flowers R Us. The return address and the story that comes with it can be anything. The object is the same, to find anyone at your mailing address that knows how to locate you.

There are two ways to protect yourself from this deception. One is to make sure that no one at your ghost address knows anything about you. The other is to use persons who, although they know you, will positively protect you. If the latter, then make sure they know about the various scams that may be used in an attempt to deceive them.

NOW FOR THE HARD PART

The hardest part of keeping your actual home address a secret is to educate your family to never, ever give out your home address to anyone other than relatives and close friends. And *even then* . . . not always, for *they* may innocently pass on your address to others. Even private investigators and policemen may have problems within the family.

Geraldine Adams, a private investigator in a southern state, specializes in tracking down corporate burglaries. (A stolen notebook computer with corporate files can fetch up to $50,000.) She had recently been responsible for a police raid and two arrests and as a result, threats had been made on her life: Both she and her husband Tom, a self-employed accountant, took these threats seriously, sold their home in the suburbs, and moved to a new and supposedly secret apartment in the city. They also changed banks and used a telephone answering service for receiving mail. One day Geraldine returned home and was stunned to find in the mail a box of new checks that her husband had ordered from the local bank. Imprinted on every check was the Adams's new residence address! (She destroyed the checks, said some unkind words to her husband, and ordered new checks herself from Checks in the Mail.)

Mateo, a police detective in Miami, was hated by innumerable bad guys he'd helped put away. For that reason, he was obsessive about keeping his home address secret. One day, while he was at work, his pregnant wife started to hemorrhage. When she could not locate her husband, she called 9-1-1. An ambulance took her to Emergency and when asked, rather than give their alternate address, she gave her actual home address.

A month later, as a result of this indiscretion, Mateo sold their home and moved.

YOUR HOUSE NUMBER

With one exception, there is no number or mailbox at any of our homes on either side of the Atlantic. There may be some local laws about displaying house numbers, but if so, I have never known it to be enforced. The reason we do not give anyone our house number is that eventually *someone will write it down*. Then they may use the address to send a thank-you note and the mail person will discover (1) who lives at that address and (2) that there is no mailbox.

Some friends of ours did let the number remain, on a house they purchased. They neglected to warn a visiting aunt that they never received mail at home. At Christmastime, she sent them a gift subscription to *Robb Report*. Guess what address she used. . . .

If you delete the number on your house but still need to have others find it, here's a little trick. If guests are coming, tell them that once they pass a certain landmark or cross street, "Watch for a house on the right with a pink flamingo on the lawn." (Don't forget to go out and plant the bird before they arrive. Extract it after they leave. They may never find the place again.)

A FINAL SOLUTION

I have a cartoon tacked on my office wall that shows a middle-aged couple in their living room, dressed to go out. The front door is open, and four large suitcases are sitting in the entrance. The husband is pouring gasoline on the carpet. The wife, who holds a can of gasoline in her left hand, is standing along one wall, talking to their daughter on the telephone. She says, "Oh, that sounds lovely, dear, but I'm afraid your father and I have already made plans." Although arson is not recommended, the following solution is.

I learned this one from a FEMA (Federal Emergency Management Agency) agent I met while staying in a motel that was near a flooded area. Two years ago he bought a $98,995 motor home under another name, and *did not license it*. This was because he didn't purchase the RV for travel purposes but for his personal residence that would only occasionally be moved. (He thus saved not only the license fees and road tax, but an $8,513.57 sales tax as well.) For $12 he got a fifteen-day permit to move it to a rural location in another state. Once or twice a year he moves it, each time getting a temporary permit. Try to find out where *this* agent actually lives!

QUESTIONS & ANSWERS

What should I do if someone sends me a registered letter?

Although some paranoid types refuse all registered mail, I am usually curious enough to accept it. However, I never sign the name that was used in the address. If there is no return receipt requested, I just scribble some meaningless lines (see Chapter 7). If a return receipt is requested, then I write *Not Here*. I have practiced the "Not-Here" signature enough times so that at first glance it just looks like a normal signature. Not once has a postal employee even bothered to look at how I signed the card. When the sender receives his card back and discovers the signature reads "Not Here," he will assume someone else had to sign because I was away . . . and perhaps I have not yet received it.

We do use our home address on our tax returns, but isn't that information confidential?

Louis R. Mizell, Jr., a former special agent and intelligence officer with the U.S. Department of State and a prolific author, tells the story of Lee Willis, a lowly clerk with the Internal Revenue Service. Willis had been stalking his ex-girlfriend for sixteen months. She thought she was safe because her home address was kept secret, her telephone number was kept secret, and she made sure her friends and neighbors kept a lookout for the stalker.

Although fifty-six thousand IRS employees have access to taxpayer files, Willis was not one of them. He did, however, persuade a coworker to run a search for him illegally. The ex-girlfriend was filing her tax returns under her true address! Willis raced to her apartment building. The lobby was locked, but he pressed all the buzzers and one of the neighbors let him in. At the last moment, the girl discovered he was in the building, called the police, and they arrested him. When they then searched Willis's car, they found a stun gun, rope, latex gloves, duct tape, and a knife.

Does that answer your question? Let's say each of the fifty-six thousand IRS employees with access to the records has five close friends, and each of these friends has five close friends of his own. Are you willing to bet your life that not one of these 1.4 million would ever commit an illegal act, or coerce another into doing so?

Is it OK to put my true home address on the bags I check when making a trip by air?

Am I not getting through here? "Do not, as long as you live, ever again allow your real name to be coupled with your home address." This includes the address on baggage tags. Baggage handlers are just as tempted by money as anyone else, and some burglars pay well for the name and address of someone who has just left on a trip. Better yet, do not check any bags at all. (See Chapter 16.)

Why would I want an out-of-state driver's license?

As a result of the stalking and murder of an actress a few years ago (the murderer got her address from the Department of Motor Vehicles), California passed a law designed to keep the information on one's drivers license private. But is it? Not according to a news broadcast on Fox TV. "The state of California," said the commentator, "earns $62 million a year selling the information on drivers' licenses to attorneys, investigators, employers, and financial institutions." As for the other forty-nine states, the general public has access to the records.

If, therefore, a private investigator wants some fast information about you, he may first try the Internet Department of Motor Vehicles. (See the Web site at www.ameri.com/dmv/dmv.htm.) For $20, he can search any one state, to bring up your address and date of birth. If he assumes you are licensed in the state where you live, his search will come up blank. He may then search the bordering states at the same price of $20 per state. If you are not there either, he may assume you do not have a license and therefore not continue with that particular search.

If you have a choice, use a distant state for your driver's license. As for whether or not to have matching out-of-state license plates, see Chapter 13.

Do I need a passport even though I have no plans to travel overseas?

Absolutely! If you do not have a passport, apply for one as soon as you have an acceptable ghost address. Use it for ID instead of your driver's license when cashing checks, identifying yourself at the airport, etc. Remember, *a passport does not show your address or your Social Security number.*

What's the best way to obtain a temporary ghost address?

Here are two methods that one of my readers uses. He writes:

"Charity Missions like the Salvation Army often have people stay there for extended periods. They accept mail for residents so they can get jobs, welfare etc. I told the supervisor that I travel a lot in and out of town and asked him if I could use the address for my personal business and gave him a $50 donation. Now, you could have someone else, say they are you, do the same thing I did, and have a great layer of protection (no cameras in those places either).

"I have done the same thing at an independently run motel. I have found that if I dress well, many of these proprietors are very sympathetic to my situation provided I am willing to pay them something for the service. The nice thing about both of these methods is that there is no PO box on the address and it's very private (cheapo motels don't often have cameras either)."

4

HOME DELIVERIES, HOUSE CALLS, BOUNTY HUNTERS, FEDEX, UPS

Shy and unready men are great betrayers of secrets; for there are few wants more urgent for the moment than the want of something to say.

—SIR HENRY TAYLOR (1800–1886), AUTHOR OF *THE STATESMAN*

George Joseph Phillips, who lives in the 600 block of South D Street in Tacoma, Washington, is a photographer. His nightmare began when he called Washington Energy Services Co. to get a new furnace and water heater installed. When work began, an employee spotted some darkroom chemicals and, apparently unfamiliar with darkroom supplies, told his boss he saw chemicals in the home that he felt might be used to manufacture drugs. A company official then notified the police. Please pay more than the usual attention to what followed, according to an article about Phillips's lawsuit in the *Seattle Post-Intelligencer* titled "Utility's house call became a nightmare":

". . . Phillips claims that after the company reported its sus-
picions to police, a member of the Police Department asked the
company to gather information from Phillips' home so police
could obtain a search warrant."

The article goes on to report Phillips's claim that the employees—yes, the ones Phillips was paying to install the furnace
and water heater—then tried to take "pictures of the home's
interior, searched through Phillips's personal effects and opened
dozens of boxes of light-sensitive paper." Further, he suspects
they also searched his computer files because his computer was
broken and beyond repair after the search. Whether or not this
was an illegal and unconstitutional search—and I think it was—
let's benefit from this shall we? The next time a worker enters
your home, think beforehand about what could possibly give him
a false impression. Then, when you let him in, stick with him.

OBTAINING CONSENT TO ENTER BY DECEPTION

The following is based on information from the January 1994
FBI Law Enforcement Bulletin, now in the public domain. This
applies to any home that federal agents would like to search, but
for lack of evidence are unable to obtain a warrant. Here is how
it works:

A van that appears to be from a well-known courier service
pulls into your driveway and the driver, with a package in hand,
rings your bell. He asks for a certain person and when you say
no such person lives at this address, he asks to use your telephone
"to call the company." If you allow him to do it, and if—while
in your home—he observes anything that *might* be illegal, he may
return within a few hours. This time he'll be with police officers
who might have a warrant to search your home, based on what
the "deliveryman" observed earlier.

You and I are law-abiding persons, with nothing to hide. Nevertheless, why invite strangers into your home? Just say no, and

give the location of the nearest pay phone. Or, if you need an excuse, here are several:

- "My husband," says the wife, "told me never to allow strangers into the house when he's not here."
- "The phone's not working right now."
- "Our only phone line is tied into the Internet."

Sometimes, of course, no warrant is needed, as the following section explains.

FEDEX, UPS, DHL, AIRBORNE EXPRESS

The only sure way to avoid having someone send you an envelope or a package by courier is to never, ever, let anyone other than your closest friends know where you really live. The result is that, should a uniformed courier show up on your doorstep—or even a clown with balloons—you automatically know that he or she doesn't belong there.

In fact, if you see someone coming up the walk—or observe them through the peephole I hope you have in your door—and do not know them, why open at all? When I was younger, cars were stolen, not hijacked, but improvements in car alarms have brought about a change. The same is starting to be true with house burglaries, now that locks and burglar alarms have improved. Thugs may just ring your doorbell. When you open, they slam their way in. Housejacking started in New York some years ago, and it will soon be coming to a city near you.

Now then, just in case you consider some of my advice to be extreme—and I confess that many do—I am willing to discuss some options. I don't recommend them, but better half an ounce of prevention than none at all.

Home delivery: Remember the cardinal rule? "Do not, as long as you live, ever again allow your real name to be coupled with your home address." If then, you are going to have a delivery made to where you really live, it must not be in your name. All courier companies keep a national database of names and addresses and countless thousands of their employees can run a search of your name. PIs know this, and many have contacts inside these companies.

If, in fact, you have *ever* received a letter or package at your present address and under your real name, the only way to protect your privacy is to move. Once this move has been made, and if you are determined to have delivery made at your home, then it must be in another name. When you sign for the courier, you sign the other name.

You may get by with no problems doing this, as long as you do not order expensive items from out of state. If you do, however, keep in mind that in states with a sales tax, it is not uncommon for irate neighbors to call the tax department and report that the people next door are buying such-and-such to avoid the state's sales tax. (You do know, do you not, that you are obligated to "voluntarily" pay the local sales tax on merchandise purchased from out of state?)

The logical solution to anonymity with courier services would seem to be to have your parcels come into one of their nearby offices and just pick them up there. Unfortunately, these companies do not employ logic. Whereas they never ask for ID at a private home, they absolutely demand it if you stop by one of their offices to pick anything up. I have argued this point in vain with the various home offices, pointing out that if I send a package in a certain name, I will sign a waiver to the effect that they may deliver to any person asking for it in that name. After all, this is similar to item number eight on all FedEx labels, which reads RELEASE SIGNATURE. *Sign to authorize delivery without obtaining signature.* In fact, if you really wish to remain incognito, have the sender sign on the line for this release and when you see the FedEx truck arrive, do not answer the door.

But do not pick up at their office. I sent an e-mail to the FedEx main office, pleading for permission to send a letter to one of my clients who would not present ID when he picked it up at an office in Memphis. I received this reply, short but not sweet:

> *Thank you for your inquiry. FedEx requires a valid consignee name and phone number for shipments that are held for pick-up. More hold for pick-up information can be found on our website at:*
> *http://fedex.com/us/services/conditions/domestic/hold.html*
> *Thank you for your interest in FedEx.*
> *Susan Carr*
> *FedEx Webmaster*

Mail-Drop Pickup: Although USPS regulations require two forms of ID in order to receive mail at a commercial mail-receiving agency, FedEx, UPS, and other couriers services are not bound by these regulations. So then, you can receive a shipment in your name or in a business name without showing ID. Here's how it works:

Assume I live in Plano, Texas. I wish to have a friend from New York City send me a small box that will not be identified with me in any way. Not by my name, and not by my address. I look up Mail Boxes Etc. in the yellow pages, choose one of the six offices listed, and have my wife make the call. The conversation goes like this:

"Hello, this is Mary Johnson with Triple-R Services in New York. I wish to send a small box to your address, for pickup by one of our salesman traveling through. Will that be satisfactory?"

"No problem—in whose name will it be?"

"We'll just send it to your address in the name of Triple-R Services. Anyone that asks for a package in that name can pick it up."

"There is a small pickup fee, of course . . ."

"No problem."

I then call my friend, who ships the package. The following week I stop by and pick up the box. (I had my wife make the call so that when I ask for the box, the manager does not recognize my rather odd accent and connect it with the "New York" caller.) Or, I can send anyone else around on my behalf, anyone at all.

ROBBERS MAY IMPERSONATE THE POLICE

If no one knows where you live, it is extremely unlikely that police will ever show up at your door. If, therefore, you see what *appear* to be policemen coming up your walk (or seen through your peephole), do not open the door. Call the police department, or even 9-1-1 on your cell phone, to check them out.

Several years ago, two men who identified themselves as police officers entered a home in a Los Angeles suburb and tied up the couple who lived there. Both wore dark clothing and caps with the word "POLICE" on the brow. They then stole a thousand dollars in cash and a laptop computer.

"Unfortunately, this happens too often," said LAPD spokesman Lt. Anthony Alba, "but generally on the eastside or the southside of town, where recent immigrants might not be familiar with our law-enforcement officials. This one's a bit different." He referred to the fact that the victims were from a relatively quiet street in a predominantly middle-class neighborhood.

Later, two Los Angeles men suspected of committing more than eighty home-invasion robberies were arrested and a press conference was held. Among the more than one hundred items confiscated from the men's home were night-vision goggles, official Los Angeles police badges, handcuffs, five handguns, a sawed-off shotgun, an assault rifle, and hundreds of rounds of ammunition.

In summary, a ghost address will give you not only protection but peace of mind as well. No longer will you have to wonder about who is coming to your door. If it is not someone you recognize, then—since no one else has this address—they have no business there. The postman? Ignore him! Woman dressed in

a FedEx uniform? Ignore her! Two or three guys with leather
jackets? Don't even *think* of answering the door! (See how easy
it is, once you eliminate all traces of your home address?)

QUESTIONS & ANSWERS

Can a bounty hunter legally break into my home?

If you ever post bail via a bondsman, and fail to show up in
court, then the answer is YES, INDEED. There have been a
number of articles and programs about this fact. As reported on
the CBS program *60 Minutes*, a bounty hunter—unlike the
police—can search whatever he likes without a warrant. He can
break down doors, read mail, boot up computers, copy keys,
whatever. The justification for all this is that anyone arranging
bail through a bondsman signs a contract, and the bounty hunter
is merely fulfilling the fine print in said contract. So if any of you
readers ever forfeit bail, you'd better make sure your home
address is *really* private.

A more likely danger is that, knowingly or unknowingly, you
invite someone into your home that has forfeited bail. This might
be a relative, a close friend, maybe even your brother, or grown
son or daughter. You might wish to give this some thought, the
next time a certain someone "stops by." In some cases, there is
a danger even in *knowing* the persons the bounty hunters are
after. One person interviewed on the *60 Minutes* program told
of a couple being held and grilled for eleven hours by bounty
hunters intent on getting enough information to track down
someone this couple knew.

If someone pounds on your door and yells "Special Agent!"
you are about to meet one or more bounty hunters in person.
Do not be fooled by the fact they may wear uniforms, carry
badges, and at first glance appear to be with the FBI or the ATF.
Or, they may get you to open the door by dressing as an
employee of UPS, FedEx, or the U.S. Postal Service. In one case,

the hunters determined that one particular tough quarry—who was wise to all normal ruses—had a young daughter whose birthday was coming up. They waited until that day, then sent in a clown with balloons. He passed muster with the closed-circuit video, the door was opened, and you can guess the rest.

We are about to move to another state. Is it safe to use a mover such as Allied, Bekins, or Mayflower?

Not if you value your privacy. Most—if not all—interstate moving services keep computer records and PIs know and use this. Keep in mind that even though you give the movers a different name, the computers can be searched by address as well. If, therefore, an investigator tracks down your present address and discovers you have moved, he will have an accomplice check the records to see what name you used, and the destination street address.

When we move—which is more often than my wife would like—I pay a driver to rent the largest size Ryder truck in *his* name. I then look under "Movers" in the yellow pages. There is usually a subsection called "Student Movers," self-employed husky young men that load and unload trucks for an hourly wage. They load the truck, the driver drives it, and at the destination another set of student movers unloads it. My driver then either drops off the truck in a nearby city, or drives it back to the city of origin. Ryder puts everything into their computers, but what do they have? Certainly not my name, and neither the previous street address nor the new one. Incidentally, you will often save a bundle of money with this method.

An alternative solution is to arrange for the Mother of All Moving Sales. Then buy a one-ton pickup and a fifth-wheel travel trailer. License each in a separate company, as discussed in Chapter 12, and be on your way in total privacy.

What about the cleaning lady or the carpet cleaner?

At the very least, use someone that your friends have used for years and will recommend without reservations. However, if you have secrets to protect, this precaution may not be enough. PIs have been known to offer serious money to obtain trash from a home office before it has been shredded.

My next suggestion may be worth far more to you than the price you paid for this book. Use someone who is an unusually active member of the Seventh-day Adventists, Jehovah's Witnesses, or the Church of Jesus Christ of Latter-day Saints (Mormons). Unlike those from mainstream religions, you will seldom if ever find a longtime member of these three religions in jail unless—as in some countries—they are there for their faith. These people believe their Creator is watching them and most would rather die than steal. The only problem is, will they want to clean your home or your carpet?

Of the three groups, I am least familiar with the Adventists. I suggest you contact the pastor of a nearby SDA church, explain what you are looking for, and ask if any members do cleaning work. If they do, tactfully ask how long they have been Adventists and how active they are in the church.

If you contact the Mormons, note that they refer to one another as "LDS," or Latter-day Saints. Howard Hughes used Mormons for bodyguards and trusted them completely. I would also trust certain ones in financial matters, such as for hawala banking (see Chapter 14). By "certain ones," I mean those that have demonstrated their faith by being missionaries in a foreign land for two years. The only problem here is that not many LDS are into cleaning. They lean more toward commercial enterprises.

A little-known fact about Jehovah's Witnesses is that in many cities they do 80 percent of the nightly cleaning in office buildings and an even higher percentage in clinics. They also do much of the cleaning in upscale homes where security is especially important. There are three reasons for this:

1. They prefer to work late at night or very early in the morning so they are free to attend three meetings a week and three conventions a year. They usually clean for a flat rate, work fast, and earn from $20 to $40 an hour.

2. A number of them have carpet-cleaning businesses and many will accept any honorable work, however humble.

3. They are so well-known for honesty that word of mouth keeps them in constant demand in the janitorial field.

Although we would be happy to employ LDS or Mormons in any of our homes, in actual practice we usually end up with Witnesses. Although they call their church buildings Kingdom Halls, we look them up in the yellow pages under "Churches." Over the years, we have learned that the best time to call a Kingdom Hall is between 6:45 and 7:10 on a Tuesday, Wednesday, or Thursday. This is just before they have one of their meetings. Ask to speak to one of the elders. If they are busy, leave your number and have them call back. When an elder comes on the line, do not use a title such as pastor or Reverend—they do not use titles. Just explain what you need.

There is no need to be embarrassed about calling. Non-Witness persons often call Kingdom Halls to ask who is looking for work. (Besides janitorial, they are in demand where large sums of money are being handled.) If you are unusually concerned about privacy, say that you prefer a worker who is a "pioneer." This is the term Witnesses use for those who put most of their time in the Bible-teaching work. They cannot be pioneers unless they have an excellent reputation both within and without their congregation. And not to worry—they won't preach to you while on the job!

What about letting a baby-sitter into our home?

If the baby-sitter is Grandma, there should be no problem. Other than that, tune your radio into the *Dr. Laura Schlessinger Show*. Better yet, call Dr. Laura. Ask her what she thinks about abandoning your little trolls to a sitter. (Best to be sitting down for the answer.)

Even if you survive the phone call and are determined to call in a sitter, do you still harbor vague fears? Then spend about $60 for a voice-activated tape recorder with multiple pickup microphones. You may hear phone calls, boyfriends coming to visit, or sounds of child abuse. A better solution is to install a nanny-cam and see what goes on in living color. Perhaps she is checking out your computer or going through your drawers!

Actually, however, if you suspect the sitter may need electronic surveillance, your fears are probably justified. Find someone else or bring in Grandma.

5

UNTRACEABLE TRASH,
ANONYMOUS UTILITIES

Satisfaction Guaranteed or Double Your Garbage Back
—GARBAGE TRUCK, CAMBRIDGE, MASSACHUSETTS

This is a short but vital chapter, absolutely essential in order to achieve your goal. Let's start out with an opportunity for you to play detective. See if you can solve the mystery.

A bilingual private investigator in San Jose, California, takes a call from a law firm in San Diego. They wish to locate a certain Victor R—in order to serve a subpoena in a civil lawsuit. They have only three pieces of information:

1. Victor, who was born in Ameca, Jalisco, is staying with friends from his home town. They live "somewhere" near Lake Tahoe, on the California-Nevada border.

2. Victor has a younger brother named Fernando who rents a one-bedroom unit in a sixty-four-unit apartment complex in San Jose. However, the PI is *not* to contact Fernando because if he does, Fernando will tip off his brother.

Worse, the lawyers want fast results and yet they put a limit on what the PI may spend. If he needs any helpers, he will have to use slave labor. The intrepid PI takes the job, despite the following drawbacks:

- If Victor is with friends, there is no way to track him down via rental agreement, telephone, or utilities.
- There are more than ten thousand Latinos in the Lake Tahoe area and nearly 80 percent of them come from the same place: Ameca, Jalisco (Mexico).
- A quick check shows that there is no telephone at Fernando's apartment.

Our intrepid PI is on the job that very evening, prepared for action. What he wants is every bit of the garbage and trash that leaves Fernando's apartment for the next thirty days. He observes that there are two large Dumpsters near the entrance of the parking lot, and learns that they are dumped between 3 and 4 A.M. every day. There is no uniformity in the bags the residents are using. Some are paper, some are white plastic bags from the supermarkets, and some are large black trash bags. The PI knows of a Guatemalan family where three teenagers are desperate for work, any kind of work, even diving into Dumpsters.

Here is where you get to play detective.

How will his Guatemalan friends know which garbage belongs to Fernando?

[Take five, see if you can guess the answer. This is not rocket science.]

Okay, check your answer with what happened next. Late that evening, the PI went from door to door, calling at each of the sixteen apartments that were on Fernando's floor. He wore a uniform with a name tag and presented each renter with a free supply of thirty trash bags, speaking Spanish or English as the occasion warranted.

"This is part of an experiment by our company," he said with a disarming smile. "The idea is to see if these extra-strong bags will cause less spillage when our trucks unload at the processing plant. If you and your neighbors use these bags for the next thirty days, we may continue to furnish them at no charge."

A young, pregnant woman answered the door at Fernando's apartment. He gave her the pitch and handed her the bags.

"*Muchas gracias,*" she said. "*Muy amable.*"

"*No hay de qué. Qué tenga un buen día.*" Have a nice day.

Then the three Guatemalans got their assignment. They were to take turns drifting past the Dumpsters both morning and evening, checking to see if there was a bag from Fernando's apartment. For every bag they brought in, the PI would pay them $20 cash. If he found what he was looking for, there would be a $100 bonus.

In the next two weeks, they brought in nine bags and were paid $180. Two days later they brought in the bag that paid a $50 bonus—Fernando had a cell phone, and he had tossed the statement in the trash after tearing it up. Pieced together with tape, it showed six long-distance calls to the same number at Zephyr Cove on the Nevada side of Lake Tahoe. That was all it would take to track down Victor, at a cost of $230 to the kids and $96 for the bags.

Have you already guessed how the kids knew which bags to pick up?

Yes, it was just as you thought. At fifteen doors, the PI gave away dark green bags. At Fernando's door, he handed over dark blue bags.

That was the windup. Here comes the pitch.

To paraphrase Johnnie Cochran:

> If it can be read
> Then you must shred.

WHAT YOUR TRASH REVEALS ABOUT YOU

Trash is not the remains of food. That is garbage. Trash is everything else. Unfortunately, the two may be mixed unless it is coming from an office building. Trash is to a detective what a gold nugget is to a prospector. Just imagine—if you dare—what investigators would have learned about you and your family if they had secretly gone through your trash for the last ninety days. We shall assume they started with a blank sheet, having no idea as to the occupants of your home. To put a picture together, they would have watched for any of the items in the following list. If anything were torn up, it would have been pieced back together.

- Bank statements with your name, address, account number, etc.
- Telephone bills with your number, and the long-distance calls you made.
- Utility and other bills, showing the name and address you use for those.
- Credit-card statements and receipts, invoices, automatic teller receipts.
- Paycheck and/or money order stubs.
- Empty bottles from prescription medicine, with your doctor's name.
- Personal and business letters. All address labels.
- Scraps of paper that might reveal a name or phone number.
- Matchbooks. Inside covers checked for phone numbers.
- Anything to indicate drug use, including triangular scraps of paper.
- Itemized grocery and pharmacy slips, for evidence of alcohol, illness, condoms, birth-control pills, or anything to indicate homosexual activity.

- Classified ads from newspapers, to see if anything is circled.
- Magazines, travel brochures, or anything that would indicate interest in weapons, strange practices, or overseas connections.

What else can you think of, in your particular case? Or that of your friends, relatives, or even your children?

Do you have a weekly arrangement for a woman to come in and clean? Does she have access to the trash?

If you work in an office, who handles the trash? Did you know that in some cases, janitors are bribed to turn trash from a specific office over to private investigators? Or—worse!—government agents?

Most likely, if you do everything else right, no one will be able to sift through your trash because they cannot find you in the first place. But *if they do* (perhaps by following you home), then make sure all papers have been shredded and that there is nothing further to be revealed from your trash.

UTILITIES

By utilities I mean the companies that furnish electricity, garbage pickup, water and sewer connections, and natural or propane gas. (Telephones will be discussed in Chapter 8.) Never give your true name—much less your SSN or date of birth!—to a utility company, nor to any other private company that will furnish a service at your actual residence.

Rather, if you own your home in the name of a trust, give each company the name of the trust and insist that the name in the company database is in the name of the trust only. In fact, do not give them your own name under any condition. Try a fictitious one, or use the wife's maiden name. Even then, this should just be her middle initial plus last name. Do not furnish her Social Security number or date of birth.

A quick and dirty method of setting up the utility accounts on short notice is to use a nominee, someone that will act on your behalf. (See Chapter 9.) Usually, the utility company will demand a cash deposit in lieu of being able to check your credit by using your Social Security number. Fine, give them a money order or a bank check for the deposit. It will be returned to you after one year of on-time payments. Make sure that the bills *never* come to your home address. Give them your ghost address, explaining that (a) you do not have a mailbox at the street address and (b) all bills are paid from your "business" (ghost) address.

What has been accomplished? Just this: If a private investigator—acting on behalf of a stalker or working with a law firm or insurance company—starts searching for you, one of the first places he will check (after cable TV) will be the utility companies. If your name is in any database, the PI will obtain the address. But as long as your name never shows up, the search will be in vain.

QUESTIONS & ANSWERS

How can I get rid of trash other than by shredding it?

If you have a fireplace or a wood-burning stove, perhaps you can burn it. Otherwise, toss your statements, bills, etc. into a box that is reserved for this purpose. Be sure to include all envelopes that indicate your name and ghost address. (Don't forget the junk-mail offers.) Then cut through the addresses and put one half of each address in one pile, the other half in a second pile. Bundle them up and toss the piles in separate public trash bins.

6

YOUR SOCIAL SECURITY NUMBER AND DATE OF BIRTH

My Social Security number? If you insist . . . 078-05-1120.

—FUTURE QUOTE FROM YOU, THE READER

In 1973, George Norman left Denver, Colorado, in a borrowed car. He was skipping out on an impending two-year prison sentence for embezzling some $500,000 from the now-defunct Rocky Mountain Bank. Over the years he ran this "starter money" into $50 million by legal means, dabbling in oil in Houston and starting software companies in Oregon and Utah.

Although he knew that U.S. marshals were after him, rather than move to Mexico or Canada he stayed in the United States, relying on alternate names to protect him. Some of the names he used were George Larson, Max Morris, George Irving, Frick Jensen, Gunner Isoz, J. Blankman, and Dr. James Hill.

Had private parties been employing detectives to pursue him, the money would have run out before many years had passed.

However, with government agents, money does not run out. Twenty-three years passed before Norman, for whatever reason, felt compelled to give out a Social Security number. Rather than use his own, or invent one, he used the number of a person he knew was dead. This Social Security number came up on a government computer as that of Tom Dangelis, red-flagged as George Norman's wife's Donna's deceased grandfather! The result was this headline in the Sunday, December 1, 1996 *Los Angeles Times*: "FUGITIVE MILLIONAIRE NABBED AFTER 23 YEARS ON THE LAM."

Yes, Norman needed catching, and they caught him. But the point is, privacy isn't only for criminals, it's also desirable for white-hat folks like you and me, and this story certainly illustrates the point about not using someone else's SSN. It also tells us, as I say in chapter 1, that when the chips go down for whatever reason, your first priority may be to gain time to sort things out.

However, a Social Security number is not the only way to quickly track you down—your *date of birth* is another:

DATE OF BIRTH

No matter how common your name, you can be quickly identified in a database by coupling either your name *or* your birth date with your address. Keeping your true home address a secret has already been discussed. As for a birth date, I seldom give out any date whatsoever.

For instance, just a few days ago I stopped in at a shopping mall to have my eyes tested. The doctor's assistant handed me a long form to fill out, asking among other things my address, telephone number, Social Security number, and date of birth. I explained that I did not live in the area, did not give out my SSN, and my age was in the "early seventies." No objection was raised. During the exam, the doctor asked me what I did for a living.

"I'm a writer."

"Oh? What do you write?"

"Articles and books about keeping your private life *private*. Which is why I didn't give you a Social Security number or a date of birth."

"Oh well," replied the doctor, "except for insurance cases, I don't need that stuff on the form anyway!" (But they don't tell you that when they hand you the form, right?)

My next stop was nearby, at one of those national chains that have optical shops in malls. I picked out the two frames I wanted and the young salesclerk started to fill in the form.

"Address?" she said.

"No local address, I live in Spain." After a puzzled look, she wrote down the address of the store itself.

"Telephone number?"

"Sorry, no telephone." She wrote down the number of the store.

"Date of birth?"

"Why on earth," I said, "would the purchase of two pairs of glasses require a date of birth?"

"The date of birth is how we identify our customers."

"I do not wish to be identified." Long pause. Then she left it blank. The next question of the form was for a Social Security number but at that point the girl just shrugged and didn't even ask me.

Personally, I enjoy these challenges, but some of my clients do not. In fact, they hate confrontations of any kind. Often, if filling in a form yourself, you can just write "legal age." Another alternative is to give a fictitious month and day, and a year a bit before or after the real one. If you feel obligated to give a date of birth, choose one that is easy to remember, such as a national holiday. Make yourself a few years younger at the same time.

YOUR SOCIAL SECURITY NUMBER (SSN)

The Privacy Act of 1974 (Pub. L. 93-579, I section 7) requires that any federal, state, or local government agency that requests your Social Security number must tell you four things:

1. Whether disclosure of your SSN is required or optional.

2. What statute or other authority requires this number.

3. How they will use your SSN, once they have it.

4. What will happen if you do not provide them with your SSN.

So then, if you are asked for your SSN by any federal, state, or local government agency (including any state university that accepts federal funds), look for the Privacy Act Statement. If it isn't there, ask to see it before you give your number. (Failure to provide a SSN will not prevent you from getting a passport, for example.) Since the subject of this book is privacy, not tax evasion, I see no problem in furnishing your SSN to the Internal Revenue Service.

YOUR DRIVER'S LICENSE

Public Law 104-208, passed in 1996, imposes an unprecedented threat regarding driver's licenses. Section 656 provides that since October 1, 2000, federal agencies will not accept for any identification-related purpose a driver's license issued by a state unless the license contains a Social Security account number that can be read visually or by electronic means. (Because of strong public objections, Congress placed a one-year moratorium on implementation of this provision, pushing it ahead to October 1, 2001.)

It appears that a few states—for now—will continue to allow an "alternate number" based on your SSN. The state has a formula for converting that number back into the SSN. Thus the

SSN is at least hidden from most nongovernmental agencies that will ask to see, or even photocopy, your driver's license. Check with your local Department of Motor Vehicles (in some states called the Department of Safety or something similar) for additional information.

Actually, apart from the state agency that issues driver's licenses, there's not much of a problem when dealing with government agencies. It's the *private* organizations that can give you industrial-strength depression. The low-level clerk behind the counter expects you to fill out that form *completely*. After all, "everyone else does," and it's "the company policy." So let's consider some of these private agencies or organizations:

YOUR EMPLOYER

If you work for wages, the IRS requires the employer to get your SSN. Sometimes they will ask for it before you're hired, so they can check your credit and criminal (if any) record. Tell them you'll give your SSN if and when actually hired for the job. If this is not acceptable, ask yourself, "How badly do I want this job?"

If you do take the job, know that your name, address, and Social Security number must by law go into the database for the National Directory of New Hires within twenty calendar days. This applies to virtually every person who is hired in the United States. The only wiggle room here is with the address. Remember the rule? "Do not, as long as you live, ever again allow your real name to be coupled with your home address." Therefore, you will give your employer only your ghost address.

In some cases, you may be able to work as an independent contractor and thus avoid giving out your Social Security number. This is easier than it used to be because in 1998, the IRS burden-of-proof rules were changed in the independent contractor's favor. If you think you might qualify as an independent contractor, consult a CPA.

HOSPITALS AND DOCTORS

If you qualify for Medicare *and wish to use it*, you'll need to furnish your true SSN. Other than that, I know of no law that requires your SSN to be an ID number. Insurance companies can often be persuaded to use another number in lieu of the SSN. True, the insurance companies do send information to the Medical Information Bureau (MIB), but I've been told the MIB does not use SNNs as identifiers, nor do they report SSNs when making reports.

Remember, when a private investigator has an associate search for your records in the Medical Information Bureau, many identical names may come up. His first choice for picking you out will be your date of birth, and his second choice will be whatever address he may have for you (if any). The very last thing you want on your record is a consultation that indicates a nervous disorder, a psychiatric problem, or a sexually transmitted disease. For these, pay cash and use a false name. Better yet, pop over into Canada or Mexico. If you can afford it, skip Medicare altogether and just pay all bills in cash. No personal information needed for that.

BANKS

If you must have a U.S. bank account, open it in a business name or in that of another person. When cashing checks, do not use your driver's license for identification. Rather, use your passport because:

- It does not show your Social Security number.
- It does not show any address for you, not even the state or country in which you live.
- Unlike the Department of Motor Vehicles (or whatever name it has in your state), you cannot easily be traced with your passport number.

Occasionally, after presenting my passport, I have been asked for my driver's license. I reply that I do not use my driver's license for ID. In one small town, the bank teller confessed that she had never seen a passport before! I had to point out where the number was, so she could write it on the third-party check I was cashing.

LANDLORDS

The emphasis on the last five letters is intentional, because some of them do indeed act as lords. A false SSN will not usually work here, as landlords like to check credit records and in some cases there is a statewide database that is in effect a blacklist of undesirable tenants. How badly do you want to live in the Bel-Air penthouse apartment, or (as the case may be) in that 1958 Rick-A-Tee mobile home?

You may be tempted to threaten the landlord with legal action such as discrimination, but in this case remember: Sun beats wind. Ask him or her to kindly call your previous landlord (if you dare). Or offer an extra-large deposit, interest-free, which is to be returned after one year if you prove to be the model tenant you say you are.

REAL ESTATE PURCHASES AND SALES

A Social Security number is normally required for the IRS reporting forms. One way around this is never actually to buy real estate. Rent, lease, or take options. Another is to purchase and sell in the name of an LLC. Your accountant may suggest you get a tax identification number (TIN) for the LLC. This is a number that is obtained from the IRS by filling out and submitting Form SS-4. It is used instead of a Social Security number so if you have a TIN, use that. A better solution, however, is to have a minority member of the LLC furnish his or her SSN. (If a taxable gain may result when the property is sold, discuss with your accountant how best to handle this.)

FALSE SOCIAL SECURITY NUMBERS

A federal court of appeals has ruled that using a false SSN to obtain a driver's license is illegal. Other than that, there appears to be no legal penalty for giving a wrong number as long as there is no intent to:

(a) deceive a government agency,
(b) commit fraud, or
(c) obtain a specific benefit.

If, then, you are someday asked for your SSN in an innocuous circumstance where you know this number will *not be checked*, you may be tempted to transpose two digits in the last four. (Never transpose any digits in the first three because these are state ID numbers.) "If they ever ask," you might tell yourself, "I'll just say it was an accident."

However, I do not recommend this. You have no way of knowing who the real number belongs to. What if it identifies a drug dealer, a child pornographer, or someone who died in 1975?

What I do recommend is that you either give your true number when absolutely required, or else no number at all. Nevertheless, knowing that you may someday be tempted to give a false number, here are three ways to come up with a Social Security number which, although false, will *not* identify you with anyone else.

1. Invent a number that lists the state of your choice in the first field, followed by 00 in the second field, as there are no legitimate SSNs with all zeroes in any field.

2. Start the number with 987-65- and then pick a number for the last four digits between 4320 and 4329. These are the numbers allowed for use in advertisements.

3. Fifty years ago, new wallets with a celluloid window insert came with a sample Social Security card included, and this number was always 078-05-1120. You might, therefore,

jot this number down and keep it your wallet or purse for emergency use.

There is a Web site at www.informus.com/ssnlkup.html where you can check to see if a Social Security number has ever been issued. Those listed for items one and two, above, show them to be invalid. However, when I ran the third number at this site, this was the response:

SSN 078-05-1120 was VALIDLY ISSUED between 1934 and 1951 in NY.

So then, if you give that number as your own but fear it might be checked, "remember" that you were in New York at the time. It would also be helpful to look at least sixty-four years old, as SSNs were seldom issued to children in those years.

Very important: Never use any of the above numbers with a government agency. Even lowly clerks will recognize them.

TIP

Who knows when you will:

(a) lose your purse or wallet,
(b) have it stolen, or
(c) have the contents searched, following a traffic stop?

Therefore, do not carry your Social Security card with you, nor *any* document that lists your SSN. (Since you will never again use your driver's license for identification, leave it in your car.) If you carry a health-insurance card or are under Medicare, I suggest you photocopy the card and block out the SSN. You can give your SSN to the health-care provider orally, if and when required.

OBTAINING CREDIT

In some cases it may be extremely difficult to obtain credit without revealing your number, so you'll have to ask yourself a question: *"How desperately do I need this credit?"* The correct answer should be, "Not *that* desperately!" In the *Computer Privacy Handbook,* author André Bacard quotes his grandfather's opinion of credit:

> "I'm 80 years old and free because I never owed a dime. Young people are addicted to credit. Mark my words, André. Credit will lead to a police state in America. I hope I die before then."

My Scottish father and my Norwegian mother ran their lives the same way, quoting Proverbs 22:7 to my sister and me: "The borrower is servant to the lender." The advice was sound. I pass it on to you.

RUN YOUR LIFE ON A CASH BASIS

If you truly wish to become invisible, never apply for personal credit. (There is occasionally a business exception, but credit in this case should be extended only to your corporation or limited-liability company.) We raised our children to pay cash or go without, we recommend the same to all our friends, and we stand by our own example even when discussing the International Dream: "Owning Your Own Home."

Incidentally, home ownership is overrated. It is usually cheaper to rent or lease your living quarters. Further, should disaster strike from whatever direction, as a renter you can move before the sun rises tomorrow morning. The homeowner, on the other hand, will dawdle and procrastinate, and in some cases this delay can be fatal.

Until my wife and I were in our fifties, we *rented,* period. When we finally did build our first home on Lanzarote Island, perched on a cliff fifteen hundred feet above the Atlantic, we followed the Spanish custom and paid cash for every brick and rock and block. *Un*like the Spanish way of thinking, however, we were mentally prepared to walk away and leave it if we had to. Since then we've built homes both there and in North America, always for cash, and only because we can afford this totally unnecessary luxury.

When the day comes that we can't afford to walk (or run) away and leave a house behind, we'll sell it, stash the cash, and go back to renting. In, as always, another name.

QUESTIONS & ANSWERS

Isn't giving out a false SSN a federal offense according to U.S. Code: Title 42, Section 408?

Before preparing this chapter I read 42 U.S.C 408 and also Case 94-5721 in the United States Court of Appeals for the Fourth Circuit: *United States of America v. Eunice Arnetta Harris Sparks.* I am not an attorney, so this is just a layman's opinion:

There does not seem to be any basis for a court case if there is no intent to deceive, and if no benefit is obtained. (In the above court case, the defendant purchased a car on credit, gave a false SSN, and then failed to make the payments.)

Can I get by without a passport, and still maintain my privacy?

Yes of course . . . if you never travel by air, never pay in a store by check, never cash a check at a bank, never receive a registered letter, and are never otherwise called upon to prove your age or identity. Since this may not be practical for you, let's discuss another aspect of drivers' licenses.

A recent news program on national television discussed the sale of pictures that go with state drivers' licenses. The buyer is a company called Image Data. What had previously been kept secret was now made public (i.e., that the source of Image Data's financing came from the United States Secret Service). Image Data *says* the only use for these pictures will be for businesses that accept checks. They will scan your driver's license and check the picture on the screen to be sure it is really you. Two questions arise:

(1) What use does the U.S. Secret Service have in mind for these pictures?

(2) Why was Image Data attempting to hide the U.S. Secret Service connection?

I cannot answer these questions. What I can do, however, is to continue to urge you not to use your driver's license for anything other than showing it to a policeman if you are stopped for a violation. (And do all within your power never to be stopped!)

Remember, for the past twenty years, most states have been selling the data from driver's licenses. This includes your height, weight, and "home address," none of which shows up on a passport. Also, as I have said before, if an investigator wishes to check you out, one of the first places he will check is the DMV in the state in which you live. I therefore say—once again—one of the very best ways to maintain your privacy is to obtain a passport and use it for identification.

What if a Social Security number is required for a hunting or fishing license?

Many states do require a Social Security number for registering a boat or buying a hunting or fishing license. The boat, of course, can be registered in the name of a limited-liability company (see Chapter 12). You may wish to hunt or fish in another state—one that does not require an SSN. The nonresident license will cost you more, but if saving money is important, meat and fish are available at the supermarket.

Can I just apply for a new Social Security number?

Many books have been published with advice about how to illegally obtain a new Social Security number. Some authors recommend you tell some wild story about how you were living in the jungles of New Guinea and just got back. More often, it is suggested you comb old newspapers for children who died young, and obtain—or fake—their birth certificate. These books are out of date because the Social Security Administration now requires anyone 18 or older to show up in person with original or certified documents to prove age, identity, and United States citizenship, along with positive proof that no card has ever been issued previously. There are just three exceptions. These are for:

1. Those relocated with new identities under the Federal Witness Security program.

2. Individuals who can prove they were victims of "identity theft" when criminals used their number repeatedly to get credit cards, make loans, and engage in other financial transactions.

3. Abused women who are hiding from husbands, ex-husbands, or former lovers. Until the latter part of 1999, only about 150 new numbers were granted each year. However, as of the year 2000, the Social Security Administration expects to grant new numbers much more freely. In addition to original documents establishing your age, identity, and U.S. citizenship or lawful alien status, you will be asked for both your old and new names if you have changed your name. You must also present evidence showing you have custody of children for whom you are requesting new numbers and evidence you may have documenting the harassment or abuse. The best evidence of abuse will come from third parties such as police, medical facilities, or doctors. Other evidence may include court restraining orders, letters from shelters, family members, friends, counselors, or others who have knowledge of the domestic violence or abuse. (For additional information about new numbers for abused women, go to the agency's Web site, *http://www.ssa.gov/pubs/10093.html.*)

Can I avoid giving my Social Security number on the basis of Revelation, Chapter 13?

I assume you are referring to the belief, held sincerely by some, that a Social Security number is the "mark of the beast." Is it true that in the past, several persons have won court cases objecting on religious grounds to state requirements for an SSN as a condition to receiving a driver's license. In *Leahy v. District of Columbia*, the circuit court upheld John C. Leahy's religious objection to providing his Social Security number in order to get a driver's license.

Later, five plaintiffs sued the City of Los Angeles on religious objection grounds, objecting to the state's requirement that driver's license applicants must provide a social security number as a condition of getting a license. They won the case in the state superior court, but I have since heard the state appealed that decision.

An October 25, 1997, headline in the *Los Angeles Times* said, "Religious Objections to DMV Upheld." The subtitle was, "Judge says five men do not need Social Security numbers to get licenses. They contend that the identification is the satanic 'mark of the beast.' " The article, written by staff writer John Dart, reads in part:

> In the first court decision to declare that a driver's license applicant can refuse to give the Department of Motor Vehicles a Social Security number for religious reasons, a Los Angeles Superior Court has ruled that the DMV must accommodate five men who contend that the numbers are the "mark of the beast" in the Bible's Book of Revelation. In handing down the decision, Superior Court Judge Diane Wayne said last week that the state agency could use another method of identification in light of the men's "sincerely held religious convictions . . . that anyone who uses his or her Social Security number is in danger of not receiving eternal life."

If you really, truly believe that the use of a Social Security number violates your religious beliefs, then take your stand. If you go to jail—and some have—you will be suffering for what you feel is a righteous cause. But if you are thinking of challenging the authorities and just using religion as an excuse, then I urge you to back off. Join the rest of us who do furnish the number when absolutely necessary . . . but never otherwise.

How can we maintain our privacy when we start having children, and especially when they start in school?

You are required to obtain a Social Security number for each child *that you claim as a dependent on your tax return*. The obvious solution is not to claim them as dependents.

In the public school system, the authorities demand an SSN from every student. The solution here is either home schooling or a private school. At no time do I ever say privacy is cheap, at least to begin with. (If a lawsuit—or worse—is someday avoided by the measures you have taken, then it will have been economical after all.)

Friendly tip: Raise your children to be self-employed when they leave home, so that their names will never, ever, go into the National Directory for New Hires. And just think of all the money you'll save by not sending them to college! (I am a university dropout, just like Bill Gates. I don't know about Gates, but I myself have never regretted dropping out back in the 1940s. Not for a day, an hour, or a minute.)

7

YOUR ALTERNATIVE
NAMES AND
SIGNATURES

Why be difficult, when with a bit of effort, you can be impossible?

—ANONYMOUS

Anyone can sign your name. If your attorney, CPA, or anyone else warns you that you cannot legally sign another person's name, ask them to prove it. (They will be unable to do so.) The only caveat is that the person's name you are about to sign must authorize this by telephone at the time of signature.

Example: You have the tax return for your Wyoming corporation, Oliver's Oddities, ready to mail on the due date. *Problem*: you forgot that your cousin Oliver, who is substituting for you as the sole director, will have to sign. Although Oliver is currently on an Arctic fishing trip, you reach him by telephone at the Frontier Lodge on Great Slave Lake.

"Oliver, we need to mail the tax return to the IRS today. OK if I sign your name as president?"

"Sure, why not?"

That's it. Go ahead and sign his name. All the IRS wants to see is *a* signature. My only suggestion here is that, when Oliver returns, have him sign an acknowledgment affirming for the private corporate records that permission was given via a telephone call the same day. Clip this to your copy of the return.

IF YOU *SAY* IT'S YOUR SIGNATURE, THEN IT'S YOUR SIGNATURE

Example: Your husband John is off hunting elk in the Rocky Mountains when an unforeseen emergency leaves you short of cash for Saturday night bingo. In the morning's mail comes his Social Security check. You cannot reach John because he is camping out and doesn't have a cell phone. Question: Can you sign his name and deposit his check in your joint account?

Yes, because you know that, if any question comes up later, he will acknowledge your signature as his own. Naturally, you sign the check *before* you go to the bank. (*Note:* Many husbands and wives practice signing each other's signatures for just such purposes as this, and some are skilled enough to fool any banker in the land.)

Warning: If, instead of going hunting, John ran off with that cute little secretary from the office, he will *not* want you to sign his name, in which case, repeat after me:

"*DO . . . NOT . . . SIGN!*"

You can use any number of different signatures, including illegible ones. In fact, among European businessmen, illegible is the order of the day. I used to work with a banker in Santa Cruz de Tenerife. His name was Hector Adelfonso de la Torre Romero y Ortega. This was his signature:

"But why," I'm often asked, "would anyone want an illegible signature?" Well, for signing letters to your friends, you do not want one, but why not have an alternative, illegible signature you can reproduce at will? Here are several reasons why such signatures are used so widely in Europe:

- If a copy of a secret letter comes to light, the identity of the signer will not be evident.
- For faxes, the signature is recognized only by those with the right to know.
- Bank accounts can be in the name of another person or in the name of a legal entity, and the one receiving such a check will have no clue as to the signer. (*Note:* There should be no problem, in any event, with the bank itself. Only the smallest of banks actually check signatures.)

AN ALTERNATE NAME

Why would you, a model citizen and taxpayer, ever temporarily need another name? The reasons given in many books include overwhelming debts, threatened vengeance by wrathful in-laws, a marriage gone bad, or getting on a Mafia hit list. But circumstances and situations can change in a heartbeat, and thousands of persons living a tranquil life one day have resorted to flight the next. The fact that you are right and the charges are wrong may be meaningless—just ask any lawyer if he can get you justice. The stock answer is, "How much justice can you *afford?*"

By the way, let's not call your second name an "alias"; that's only for the criminal types. What you want is a perfectly respectable alternate name, an assumed name, a nom de plume, nom de guerre, also called a pseudonym. (These can be used almost anywhere, as long as there is no intent to defraud.) Have you ever thought about being in the movies, even as an "extra"? Then you'll want a *stage name*. Or perhaps you'd like to be a writer, like Samuel Clemens, a.k.a. Mark Twain? If so, your journey will begin with the first step, choosing a *pen name*. (Women often use their maiden names in business and either men or women can adapt the British custom of using a hyphenated name. If Hillary Clinton did this, she would write her name Hillary *Rodham-Clinton* and in an alphabetical listing such a name would be under "R.") However, a pen name can be any name you like.

For privacy, nothing beats a common name because it is so hard to identify which one belongs to you. (Just ask any PI.) If your name is, for example, Meinhard Leuchtenmueller, you will want to use a much more common name where possible. Suppose you will be working out of an address in Minneapolis. Why not use something like M. Anderson for your mail-order business? (There are more than ten thousand M. Andersons in the United States, most of them in the upper Midwest.) Or, if you work out of Miami or Los Angeles, you might try M. Hernandez. Check the local telephone directories for the most common names in your area.

TITLES

A surprising number of people—even in America—have a desire for some sort of title that will make them feel important. If they wish, they can call themselves a doctor, a lawyer, a CPA, or a captain with Northwest Airlines. That is, in the United States. (Do not try this in Europe!) In the Land of the Free, it is not what you call yourself but what you practice. If you are a "CPA," do not advise anyone on taxes. If you pose as a lawyer, do not give any opinions on the law.

For many, the title of choice will be "doctor." Here are some guidelines for wanna-be doctors:

Do not give advice. Explain that you are not "that kind" of a doctor. Maybe you deal only with viruses from Chad. Also, you will certainly be truthful when—if called upon for some emergency—you say you are not in "practice" and do not therefore carry malpractice insurance. Frank Abagnale, Jr., in his intriguing book *Catch Me If You Can*, says that when passing himself off as a doctor in the state of Georgia, he had a standard answer for anyone who asked what kind of doctor he was.

"I'm not practicing right now," he said, identifying himself as a pediatrician. "My practice is in California and I've taken a leave of absence for one year to audit some research projects at Emory University and to make some investments."

However, Abagnale did not always stick to his standard answer. On one occasion, an attractive brunette mentioned an "odd, tight feeling" in her chest. He did examine her privately. His diagnosis was that her brassiere was too small.

Do not do as he did unless you are willing to risk both civil and criminal charges of assault.

It is permissible to act the part. Subscribe to a couple of medical magazines and carry one around. Wear a smock with a stethoscope in the pocket.

"You can even join the county medical society" says Jack Luger, in his book *Counterfeit I.D. Made Easy.* He says you can simply explain that you are not licensed in the state because you're doing research rather than holding a practice and that the most that can happen is they'll refuse to accept you.

A CORPORATE NAME

As this book goes to press, the state of Wyoming still allows you to incorporate in the name of a person, with no corporate identifier such as Inc. or Ltd. at the end of the name. If you choose to go this route, however, I suggest you act quickly. The Wyoming legislature has a nasty habit of changing the rules with no advance notice, and making them retroactive. (For further details, see Chapter 10.)

MEDICAL RECORDS

From a long article in the *Los Angeles Times*, February 8, 1999, under the subtitle "Some Fear Seeking Care":

> It's 10 p.m. Do you know where your medical records are? . . . Your medical records can turn up in places you'd never imagine, read by people you've never met. . . . It's hard to believe that in a country where video rental records are protected by law, medical records are not. . . .
>
> A survey commissioned by the California HealthCare Foundation . . . found that one in six Americans engages in "privacy protected behaviors," such as paying out of pocket for care otherwise covered by insurance, lying to their doctor about their medical history or being afraid to get care. . . .
>
> LaTanya Sweeney, an assistant professor of public policy at Mellon University in Pittsburgh, demonstrated how easy it is to pierce the privacy in so-called anonymous medical records. Even when names have been stripped off records that contain date of birth, sex, race and diagnostics, she can readily re-identify the individual by cross-referencing with a $20 voter registration list. . . .
>
> In one instance, she looked at data from the city of Cambridge, Mass., population 54,000, and was able to identify former Gov. William Weld because only five people in the city—and only one in his ZIP Code—had his date of birth.

The conclusions that some people may draw from articles like this are:

- Do not give the doctor a complete medical history.
- Change the birth date. Use a false Social Security number.
- Get off voter rolls and never return.

WEB SITES ADVERTISING FAKE ID

If you have an e-mail account, you are most likely getting offers to purchase either fake driver's licenses or computer programs that will generate fake ID. Or, if you search the Internet for "Fake ID," you will come up with an endless supply of offers. Because my clients kept asking me about these Web sites, I started sending in money orders to check them out. Sometimes I received a grossly inferior product. Other times I received nothing at all. Eventually I stopped losing time and money this way.

Lee Lapin, author of *How to Get Anything on Anybody—The Newsletter,* came to the same conclusion. In his September 1999 issue, referring to fake ID offers he wrote, in capital letters, "AS OF THIS WRITING I KNOW OF NO, ZERO, SITES THAT SELL ANYTHING EVEN VAGUELY WORTH BUYING!"

QUESTIONS & ANSWERS

How can I change my name legally?

This is seldom recommended. After all, you may use one or more additional names and still retain your legal name. However, to answer the question: When you legally change your name, you *abandon* your present name and choose a new one of your liking. I suggest you choose a common name, one that will be shared with thousands of others. In the USA, 25 percent of men of retirement age have one of the following names: John, William, James, Charles, or George. As for a last name, why not pick a family name from the Mayflower? Here are some of the more common names, culled from a complete list kept by Christopher Jones, Master, A.D. 1620:

Alden, Browne, Carter, Clarke, Cooke, Fuller, Martin, Priest, Rogers, Thompson, Turner, Warren, White, and Williams.

The usual rules apply (i.e., the new name may not be the same as that of a famous person, nor can there be intent to defraud). There are two methods to do this:

The use method: You simply begin using your new name everywhere. This may involve changing your driver's license, your bank accounts, and all other areas where your present name appears. Be prepared to spend some serious time with this. The biggest stumbling block may be at the DMV. At the very least, you will need to fill out a form for this purpose before receiving your new driver's license. Often you will be asked for an original document such as a birth or marriage certificate. Remember, this *use* method requires no lawyer, no trip to the courthouse, and is not legally registered anywhere.

The court method: State statutes regarding legal name changes vary, so if you dislike the requirements in one state, check those in another. A lawyer is not necessary, so do not use one; they keep records in their files. Various books on name changes are available and you may find one or more of these at your local library. A date will be set for a court appearance, and the judge will question you to make sure you are not changing your name for a deceitful purpose. If no such reason emerges, you can expect approval of your new name, and this name change will be valid in all fifty states and the District of Columbia. Remember, you have left a paper trail. There is a file in some file cabinet that contains the name you were born with.

Warning: Some name-changers have been known to bribe an employee to take their old file and accidentally "misfile" it inside another, thicker file—some old case that's long since been settled. Although that does solve the "paper trail" problem, do not do it. It is a criminal action. Some doing this have been caught. Further, it is not necessary. I have already outlined ways to use alternate names in a hundred percent legal way. Reread this chapter again.

What do you think about fake passports?

In 1992 I was offered a passport from the "Dominion of Melchizedek." I turned it down. (As you know, Melchizedek was the King of Salem, mentioned in Genesis. No country was ever named for him.) Less than a year later, I read about one of the promoters being arrested at Incline Village, on the Nevada side of Lake Tahoe. What surprised me wasn't that he was arrested— I expected that—but that before being caught he'd sold *thousands* of the fake Melchizedek passports at inflated prices. Another "country" currently being touted is Sealand.

Remember the murder of Gianni Versace? An article in the *Seattle Post-Intelligencer* headlined "Cunanan shaved his head, grew a beard," discussed Miami Beach houseboat owner Torsten Franz Reineck. I quote from paragraph eight:

> Reineck, 49, claims to be from an unrecognized nation called the *Principality of Sealand*, according to law enforcement authorities. The *Miami Herald* reported yesterday that Reineck claims to be a diplomat from Sealand, which issues its own passports. He drives a car bearing diplomatic plates from the make-believe principality, the paper said.

I never recommend false passports, not even from former nations such as British Honduras [now Belize]. Nor fake license plates. All this does is draw attention to yourself, which you do not need.

What if someone like Sears demands my name before they will sell me a large item?

First, allow me to describe my own experience with Sears. Less than a year ago, my wife and I went to a Sears store to buy an upright vacuum. The first hint of incompetence came when I asked the salesperson if I could speak to someone who thoroughly understood the differences between the models. Puffing out a more than ample breast, she assured me that *she* was that person.

"OK, fine. How many motors does this Whispertone upright have?"

"Hey, *Anna!*" she yelled, at a woman three aisles over. "How many motors in this red one?" Anna told her there were two, as I suspected. So much for this clerk's expertise. But the "red one" looked good so I said I'd take it, and would she kindly take the cash and ring it up as we were in a hurry? Here is the conversation that followed:

"Name, address, and telephone number?" she said, chubby fingers poised over the computer keyboard at the cash register.

"We live in the Canary Islands and have no local address. Besides, this is cash, remember?"

"Doesn't matter, the computer won't accept the sale without a name, address, and telephone number."

"You mean to tell me you refuse to sell me a vacuum cleaner unless I identify myself?"

"That's right, I can't sell it without putting a name, address, and telephone number into the computer."

"Call your supervisor."

The supervisor appeared out of nowhere, got the picture at a glance, and whispered to the clerk, "Type in *Sears* and pick any name whatever." So she typed in "Sears," choose the name "Dennis Searson" and as far as Sears is concerned, Dennis bought a vacuum that day. I went back to the shipping department, handed in the slip, and three minutes later the vacuum came out on a hand truck.

"Dennis Searson?" said the young man, looking around.

"Here!" I said. And that was how we got our vacuum cleaner.

And now to answer your question: Don't make waves, as I did. (For me, making a fuss is just a hobby, but my wife is still embarrassed when I say, "Call your supervisor.") Just memorize a fake name, address, and telephone number that you can rattle off with ease. Or go through an old file of business cards, pick a name you like, and carry the card. When you are asked for your name, address, and phone number, just have the clerk copy off the information on the card.

I don't have any old business cards. Where can I quickly find some?

Go to a restaurant where they have a box or bowl for business for business cards. (You drop your card in, with the object of winning a free meal for two if the card is picked in a drawing.) I know of no law that prohibits you from reaching in there and grabbing a handful. Be discreet, of course. . . .

8

TELEPHONES, ANSWERING MACHINES, FAXES, RADIOS, BEEPERS

Question: What do the police call an illegal wiretap?
Answer: A "confidential informant."

In 1977, California millionaire Gary Allen Bandy purchased land near the rural community of Gardiner on Washington state's Olympic Peninsula. He then proceeded to build a castle and other medieval buildings, bringing in artists to carve intricate Norwegian trolls on wooden posts. He was subsequently featured in the *National Enquirer* as an eccentric millionaire surrounded by his medieval buildings and trolls.

In 1991, a son was born to Gary and his wife Eva. Later, they separated, and in 1995, divorce proceedings were begun. Eva hired attorney Natalie De Maar. Gary hired attorney Steven Fields. Bitter charges flew back and forth as Gary and Eva battled for custody of son Geoff, then four.

Eva Bandy rented a home in the upscale community of Gig Harbor, at the northern end of the Tacoma Narrows bridge. The owner lived just across the street. His name was James Wilburn and he was a private investigator. What followed next was the subject of an article in the *Peninsula Daily News*:

> Bandy's attorney, Steven Fields, was leaving a voice mail message for Eva Bandy's attorney, Natalie De Maar. He was using the speakerphone. Sitting in his office was Bandy and another attorney. Fields thought he disconnected the speakerphone and proceeded to have a conversation with Bandy.

What Fields failed to realize was that the speakerphone was not disconnected. Therefore, when Bandy admitted that he had hired an investigator to put a wiretap on his wife's phone, his words were being recorded on attorney Natalie De Maar's answering machine tape. The tape eventually wound up in the hands of the FBI, who then raided Bandy's home at Gardiner Beach and his 50-foot yacht at a nearby marina. A week later, Bandy was arrested while on a trip through Idaho.

What have we learned so far?

1. Some PIs will bug cars and residences if the pay is right.

2. Some lawyers cannot be trusted with confidential information.

3. When it comes to speakerphones and answering machines, (to paraphrase Murphy's law), any mistake that can be made will be made, and at the worst possible moment.

We can learn more. Gary Allen Bandy was sentenced to two months in prison and five years of probation. He was also fined $21,138. He will be subject to drug and alcohol testing, and as a convicted felon, will be prohibited from possessing any firearms.

Attorney Steven Fields did not go to jail. There are no laws against stupidity.

The private investigator did not go to jail. The article did not say if he turned state's evidence, so I can only state a general truth: No matter how much you trust an attorney, a doctor, a CPA or a private investigator, when a prosecutor starts talking jail time, these and other professionals may give you up in a heartbeat. (The G. Gordon Liddy types are a disappearing species.)

TELEPHONE SECURITY

"Telephone security" is an oxymoron because a telephone conversation is never secure. It goes over hard lines, may be beamed up and down from satellites, or travel via digital or analog radio waves, and *it can be intercepted*. There are other ways to communicate, and thousands of privacy seekers in Europe and North America have come to the same conclusion. So here is my very best advice to you, right from the start: *Get rid of your telephones*.

If, however, you cannot imagine life without a telephone, then let us proceed to Plan B. Here are some of the questions you will have to answer, sooner or later:

- In what name will your telephone be (un)listed?
- Hard-line, cordless, cellular, and/or satellite?
- Incoming calls: forwarded from an 800 number, or from another location? Or via an alphanumeric pager?
- Will you use an answering machine and if so, with what message?
- Should you consider VHF-FM radio? Voice mail?
- What if—horror of horrors—you must call 9-1-1?

UNLISTED NUMBERS

An unlisted number is no longer the protection it used to be. Many unlisted telephone numbers now appear on the Internet as well as on the ubiquitous CD-ROM directories, and these allow for reverse searches.

Example: Your wife gets the telephone in her maiden name, Harriet Helpless. It is unlisted and has call-blocking. Nevertheless, from time to times she calls toll-free numbers. *All* toll free numbers have Automatic Number Identification (ANI) and these numbers are captured. Eventually this number will be in various databases. Then, if this number is given out to the wrong person, he or she will type the number into a ProPhone or PhoneDisc program, or check on the Internet, and come up with both her name and street address.

It may boggle your mind to know how many CD-ROM directories are out there, with thousands more being sold in the time it takes to read this section. In fact, if you have a CD-ROM drive on your computer, you, too, should purchase a phone directory from your favorite discount price club, if you haven't already done so. The two best CD-ROM phonebooks are Phone-Disc PowerFinder (800-284-8353 or 301-657-8548) and Select-Phone Deluxe from ProPhone (800-992-3766). SelectPhone is the most user-friendly, but a recent survey showed that a majority of private detectives use PhoneDisc. Either is fine, and I use both. Be sure to get the latest edition, as they are updated quarterly.

Alternatively, if you are on the Net, similar information is available at www.freeality.com.

The conclusion, then, about unlisted numbers, is that they are not secure. Always remember that if you give out a telephone number that is on a land line, a reverse search may reveal whatever name you used to obtain the service, plus the street address. Therefore, never give out such a number to those not entitled to have it.

If you list your telephone in an alternate name . . .

Use a common name that is the same as that of many other people, so that you cannot be singled out. I like first names like John, Robert, Mary, and Elizabeth, with surnames like Johnson,

Cohen, McDonald, Anderson, and Brown. Never use a middle name or initial. To see why, pick any combination of the foregoing (Mary Johnson, John McDonald, et al.) and do a search on your CD-ROM phonebook. Watch the hundreds if not thousands of duplicate names scroll by, which means your telephone name has a better chance of being lost in the clutter.

Note: How not to answer the telephone: Until the present moment, you or members of your family may have been answering the telephone with phrases such as:

"Buddy Barrington here."

"This is the Barrington residence."

"Hi, this is Betty!"

"Barrington's Invisible Inc."

However, what if the telephone company is calling, or a private detective is on the line, or a process server with a subpoena that has your name on that document in his inside sport coat pocket? A simple "Hello" or "Good morning" will suffice, or a repetition of the last four digits of the telephone number. If that stifles your spirit, try:

"Hello from the Garden City, how may I help you?," or

"Hi there, it's a great day here in Butte, Montana, let's talk!"

Let the *caller* be the one to mention a name, and when necessary, answer with a question. Let's say you're Buddy Barrington but the phone is in the name of John Johnson, the car's in the name of Ole Olson, and the house and utilities are in the name of *The Tin Man Trust*.

Caller A: "Good morning! How are you today, sir?"

You say: "What are you selling?" (When "How-are-you?" rather than your name, follows "Hello," you know it's a salesperson.)

Caller B: "May I speak to Mrs. Johnson, please?"

You say: "What is this in reference to, please?"

Caller B: "This is Cora with the Crystal County Sheriff's Department." Don't panic. Don't speak; *wait for more information*.

Caller B: "We're sponsoring the Crystal County Crusade Against Crime, and for a small donation you can—"

You say: "Mrs. Johnson won't be here for at least two months, but thank you for calling, good-bye."

Practice beforehand and in time you'll stop getting sweaty hands and an accelerated heartbeat.

ANSWERING MACHINE MESSAGES

We've all heard instructions like "Please leave a message for Buddy, Betty, or Little Boseefus." Not cool. A simple "Please leave your name, number and message at the sound of the beep" will do fine.

Some of our antisocial friends do not want messages left by anyone other than friends who know them. If we call Betty and Buddy, this is the message we get:

"Hello, glad you called the home of B, B, and Little B. We never answer in person. Please leave your first, middle, and last name, Social Security number, date of birth, street address, and telephone number. Sorry, but if you fail to leave complete information, your call will not be returned—*beeeeep!*"

If we call Nick and Amy, we get another message:

"Congratulations, you've just reached the Niccolò Machiavelli Misinformation Centre. Since we never answer in person, be sure to leave your name and number. After we've doctored the tape, your message will implicate you in a KKK plot to assassinate Supreme Court Justice Clarence Thomas and this will be brought to the attention of the FBI—*beeeeep!*"

Friends of these two couples know they can go ahead and leave a message anyway.

CHANGING YOUR LISTING

If you are not yet willing or able to move to a new location, you may still contact the telephone company to say you are moving away. (If asked, tell them you are moving to Mexico City or to London.) Set a date for the service to be discontinued.

A few days or weeks later, order a new telephone, which will of course have different numbers. If you are using a nominee—an alternative person—have him or her make the call. This person will *not* admit to having had service before.

Since no credit history is available, the telephone company will ask for a cash deposit to ensure payment. Stop by their offices or mail in a money order for the requested amount—usually a few hundred dollars. Assuming you pay your bills on time, expect your deposit to be returned to you at the end of one year.

BLOCK ALL UNWANTED CALLS FOREVER

Various companies sell units that filter out unwanted calls. One of the original ones was a unit called LineMinder, sold by LM Communications, 997 Senate Drive, Centerville, Ohio 45459. Before your telephone rings, the LineMinder intercepts the call and replies in a recorded voice:

"Hello, this is LineMinder, please enter your security code."

Your friends, of course, will know the code because you have given it to them, but strangers will not. If the caller enters a wrong number or no number at all, the recorded voice says "Security violation" and terminates the call.

When the correct code is entered, LineMinder responds, "Thank you, now ringing," and then, for the first time, you hear your phone ring.

I recently tested a similar unit, the Ad-Tec TS-300 Tele-Screen, from the Edge Co. P.O. Box 826, Brattleboro, VT 053202 for $44.95 (1-800-732-9976). It is similar to the LineMinder. When your telephone number is dialed, a female voice asks the caller to please punch in the four-digit security number. Once again, unless the correct number is then entered, the call will not go through. The four-digit code can be set to any number, and you can change it at will. However, the only ring comes from the Tele-Screen unit itself. The ringer on your telephone stays silent, and the ring from the Tele-Screen is not very loud. There must be some solution to this problem but it will be difficult to call the manufacturer because they are made somewhere in Taiwan.

CORDLESS PHONES

About two years ago, ABC television's *Good Morning America* ran a feature about the extreme dangers inherent in the use of cheap cordless phones. Charles Gibson quoted authorities that say 65 percent of all Americans have a cordless phone in the house and "90 percent of all conversations can be listened to." And many are! One unhappy cordless owner, interviewed in shadow, said he was suing the manufacturer, because the instruction booklet said his cordless phone was "secure." He was also suing the dealer, because the salesman confirmed the information that conversations would be secure. Believing what he heard and read, he then used this phone to talk about intimate details of his life with his lawyer, his doctor, and others. When a friend finally confessed to him that neighbors were scanning every conversation—and laughing!—he was so embarrassed that he sold his home and moved away.

In one sense, the ABC television program was incomplete. Suppose you watched that program and, as a result, decided not to use your cordless phone for any sensitive conversations in the future. Let's say you decide to make a really secret call to your friend George (knowing that a certain party would sue both you and George for slander if it was overheard).

Although there is only one line in your home (i.e., you have just one telephone number), you have two phone jacks, one for the cordless phone in the kitchen and the other for a normal phone in your bedroom. To avoid the cordless, you use the phone in the bedroom to make your call. Are you safe? Not necessarily.

The base unit of many older cordless phones broadcasts the incoming half of the conversation no matter which phone is picked up, so although the neighbors may not hear what *you* say, they'll certainly be able to hear every word from George, and will fill in the blanks!

If you still want cordless, purchase an upscale digital (not analog) model that transmits in the 800 or 900 MHz range. Although these *can* be scanned, they are reasonably secure because both base and handset units talk to each other in a digital code, randomly set to one of more than 65,000 codes. When I queried international scanner expert Keith C—— about the 800/900 MHz phones, he replied:

> "The spread-spectrum stuff is really hard to pick up—nearly impossible. There is also less of a chance of interference from other phones. The 900 MHz cordless phone band has quite a mix of equipment on it. Some of the digital systems would be nearly impossible to listen in on. However, there are also cheap analog phones on the 900 band so it's buyer beware. Do not be fooled by the claim of digital security codes. Analog units can have this and use the code just to establish the connection between the base and handset. It just prevents unauthorized use of your phone line."
>
> Later, Keith said:
>
> "The real question is who wants to listen? NSA could monitor any of these easily. *A private detective can probably pick up your call just from windowpane vibrations in your home* and may violate the law and eavesdrop. There is sophisticated military type stuff that can capture your keyboard strokes on your computer unless it is tempest-hardened, and high-end eavesdropping equipment like

this may be used by law enforcement and the Mafia to
serve their purposes. If you are worried about a kid with
a baby monitor or Bearcat scanner, then the 900 MHz
spread-spectrum phones probably offer enough security."

Keep in mind, then, that digital codes operate *only* between
the base and the handset, not from the line to the base unit. If,
therefore, your telephone line is tapped, digital security will be
of no help.

THE TELEPHONE AT THE OTHER END

When you make a sensitive call, do you make sure the person at
the other end is on a secure line? Earlier this year, I made a
sensitive telephone call to a certain person who lives in a large
trailer court on one of the islands in Puget Sound, Washington.
As the conversation grew more serious, she said, "Just a minute,
Jack, I'm going to switch to a more secure telephone." [*Oh-oh!*]
When she came back on the line, I learned she had been on a
portable phone, and now thought all was well because she was
using a hard-line telephone *on the same line.* When I asked her
how old the portable phone was, she said about six years. Fortunately, she and her husband also have another line for the fax
machine so she called me back on that line, and agreed to toss
the portable telephone in the trash. And listen to this: She then
told me she *knew* her calls were being monitored. She said there
were some "militia types" in the trailer court, and that some of
the neighbors had made comments about conversations she'd
had on the portable phone! Obviously I should have asked her,
"Are you on a portable telephone?" If she said no, then I should
have asked her, "Is there a portable phone on the same line?"

A more serious problem arises when you call someone whose
telephone—unknown to them—is tapped. In that case, no matter what preventive measures have been taken, you have a problem. . . .

OBTAINING A CELL PHONE

I currently use Verizon Wireless. I gave them a bank cashier's check for a $1,000 security deposit (in lieu of a Social Security number), and they handed me a new phone on the spot. This cell phone cannot be traced back to me. The bills go to a remote address and are paid from there. This phone is never turned on except when I do so to call out. Therefore it is almost impossible to locate the phone, should anyone try to do so. (When a cell phone is left on, it sends out a continuous signal identifying the nearest cell tower.) The service includes voice mail, which I check twice a day.

Here is another way: Get a nominee—someone who is willing to use his Social Security number, pay him $100 (or whatever it takes) for the effort, and have this person get the telephone, giving one of your ghost addresses so you receive the bills. (Make sure that mail will be received in his name, along with whatever other names you are using there.)

A faster, easier way: Use a prepaid cell phone service such as Tracfone (www.tracfone.com). No credit checks are required and your name will not be linked to the telephone. You can purchase them at K-Mart, RadioShack and JC Penney.

Coming soon: *disposable* cell phones!

SCANNING A CELL PHONE

It is often thought that cell phones are reasonably secure because U.S. law prohibits the sale or import of scanners that do not have some of the frequencies blocked. However, there is no such law in Canada. The result is that PIs and others smuggle in unblocked scanners, and thus the danger remains. However, if you yourself are thinking of obtaining an unblocked scanner, please note:

Many scanners sold in Canada *are* blocked because they were manufactured in the United States. I recently spoke with the manager of a RadioShack store in Surrey, BC. He said the scanners in his store all came in from RadioShack in the States and were therefore blocked, even though Canadian law does not prohibit him from carrying unblocked Unidens if he wishes to do so. One store that does sell unblocked scanners is Durham Radio Sales and Service Inc., 350 Wentworth Street East, Unit #7, Oshawa, Ontario, Canada. Phone 905-436-2100. If you are on the Net, try www.durhamradio.com/ar8200.htm.

I checked with the owner of this store. He will sell to me across the counter, but will not ship to the States since the United States prohibits such imports. I then checked with UPS, to see if I might ship one of the scanners to a certain address south of the border as a "gift" and list it as a walkie-talkie. They handed me a copy of the form that must be filled out. A signature is required after these words: "I certify that all of the information given above is true and complete."

I was not prepared to sign this false statement, much less try to sneak a scanner across the border. In fact, when I did cross the border—sans scanner—the Customs officer asked me what I had purchased in Canada, and I named the items. When it appeared I could then drive on, he suddenly barked, "Did you buy *anything else?*" I was relieved to be able to say truthfully that no, I had not.

Later, I managed to track down a Canadian electronics expert on the Internet. He recommended I purchase a perfectly legal (cell-blocked) Uniden Sportcat 150. He claimed it would do a good job receiving cellular on "image" frequencies. (This means that in addition to broadcasting on the assigned frequency, the phone may accidentally send a second signal on another—unauthorized—frequency. Image frequencies show up when good design is compromised in the name of cutting costs.) The scanner will pick up cell phone frequencies quite by accident on frequencies assigned for other purposes. (Cellular phones are not transmitting on frequencies they are not assigned to. Rather, the scanner picks up the chosen frequency and the cell frequency simultaneously. I was told that if I searched the 800 MHz band, I would hear cellular.)

I then located a Sportcat on the Internet for $159.95 plus shipping, in order to test his claims. Once I figured out how to run it, I scanned the unblocked area of the 800 MHz range. Yes, it did indeed pick up cell-phone conversations—including one by my wife!

This does not mean that the bad guys are out there night and day, searching for your cell-phone conversations. It does mean, however, that you should think twice before having any sensitive conversations, and in any event you should never identify your-self by your full name.

TRACING A CELL PHONE

The *Los Angeles Times*, in a recent article discussing so-called privacy protection for the next-generation digital cellular tele-phones, had this to say:

> Bruce Schneier, a well-known expert on code breaking, and other researchers, have found a way to easily monitor any numbers dialed on a digital telephone, such as credit card numbers or passwords. In addition, they say, voice conversations can easily be deciphered. The findings could be a setback for the telecommunications industry, which has touted the security features of the new digital cellular and PCS systems.

Yes, cell phones can be traced to your general location, as O. J. Simpson found out when he was in the white Bronco. But if the police and/or a federal agency are about to go after you, then you've got better things to do than to read this section. Skip straight to Section 10, *Anonymous travel in North America*, and study the part about crossing the border.

Beginning not later than October 1, 2001, wireless carriers must—in theory—pinpoint the location of each caller to within

388 feet. Whether they can actually do that in rural areas with few cell towers remains to be seen. In any event, I often prefer a cellular phone to a hard line for the very real reason that it is *not tied to a physical location*. In fact, you may wish to use a pager in tandem with your cellular telephone. (As long as your cell phone is turned off, it cannot be targeted.)

- Give out only your pager number.
- When you receive an alphanumeric message that you wish to respond to, turn on your cell phone and call back.

Among other things, this will solve the problem of having your batteries run down when your cell phone is on all the time.

Pagers (also called beepers): Many pager companies are not as strict as the telephone companies, but if they are, there is always the alternative of using another person's name. Two companies worth considering are PageNet and SkyTel. The alphanumeric pagers don't just beep; they send a visual message to your pager wherever you may be.

Persons wishing to contact you call an 800 number with a live operator. They give the message to the operator, who types it into a computer, from which it is sent to the pager. If you happen to have a SkyCell 2-Way, the sender can give you multiple choices and you can respond by number.

SATELLITE TELEPHONES

You'll see these advertised in yachting magazines. They were developed for oceangoing ships but some airlines use them now for passengers. You can use them anywhere, even in an isolated mountain valley or in a trackless desert. However, the rates are extremely high and the entire industry is in a state of flux. The

FBI is determined to find a way to monitor satellite telephones and by the time this is published they may be able to do so.

VHF–FM RADIO

For years I have been carrying a pair of Standard HX250S VHF radios—the marine equivalent of a CB radio, but without the clutter. The FCC used to require a license to run these radios, but at the present time no license is required.

Almost any VHF-FM radio can be special-ordered with a scrambler that encrypts the transmissions. They must be ordered in pairs and are popular among commercial fishermen who wish to keep others from knowing what the catch is and where it's located. You, however, do *not* want a scrambler because:

- All Coast Guard stations automatically unscramble all conversations, and
- If a normal conversation is overheard, it won't attract attention, whereas a scrambled message may do just that, and in any event,
- If you are stopped and searched for any reason, you might pass off a regular radio as one you normally use when "renting a fishing boat," but can you imagine explaining a scrambler by saying you are a commercial fisherman?

These radios are legal to use from boat to boat, or from boat to shore, but not from land to land. The Coast Guard monitors VHF calls, especially channels 9 and 16, so use other channels. Even if they do overhear you, they may not try to locate you as long as you avoid buzzwords like bomb, drugs, rape, and cash.

Should you decide to use a VHF-FM in whatever location, remember that just one party speaks at a time. You push a button when you are speaking, and release it when you finish. You would decide beforehand which channel to use, avoiding 9 and

16. The correct form is to first state the name of the boat you are calling, followed by your boat name, like "*Pretty Baby*, this is *Liquid Assets*." You would then wait for an answer. Under no circumstances will I admit that any of the following conversations have ever taken place while tooling south on I-5, leading the way for a friend behind me in a Ryder truck:

> HYDROTHERAPY, THIS IS STRESS RELIEF. CHECK OUT THE
> TWO BLONDIES IN THE BEEMER CONVERTIBLE.
> LAWSUIT ONE, THIS IS LEGAL LOOPHOLE. THROTTLE
> DOWN FOR SMOKEY BEHIND THE PINE TREES.
> PLEASURE ISLAND, THIS IS DEBT MAN'S FLOAT. PULL
> INTO PEA SOUP ANDERSONS AT THE NEXT INLET.

Lower in power but completely legal are the new UHF, ½- watt Motorola TalkAbout radios that provide dependable two-way communication up to two miles. Check with your local RadioShack store.

Note: When you shop at RadioShack, ignore their pleas for a "last name" and/or "the last four digits" of your telephone number. If you tell them you do not want your name in their computer, they will still allow you to hand over your money. (Despite many of customer complaints about this, most RadioShack stores continue this irritating practice.)

However, some clerks do get obnoxious if you bring something back for a refund. When I recently returned some expensive audio cables (having found cheaper ones at Wal-Mart) and presented my sales receipt, the clerk asked for my name.

"I do not wish to have my name in your computer."

"We cannot refund money without a name. Your name?"

"John Johnson," I said—one of my standard generic names.

"Address?"

I made one up.

"Telephone number?" What would he ask for next, a Social Security number?

"No telephone."

"I beg your pardon?"

"*I . . . do . . . not . . . have . . . a . . . telephone*," I said through clenched teeth.

I got my refund, and a Radio Shack employee had created yet another case of customer ill will.

HAM HANDHELDS

The word "Ham" was the station call of the first amateur wireless station operated by some amateurs of the Harvard Radio Club in 1908. Now, of course, Ham refers to all amateur radio. Although marine frequency VHR radios are effective for most applications and cheaper than many Ham handheld systems, their frequency range is admittedly limited. Also, in some maritime areas, the channels may be crowded.

Although a Ham handheld can be tracked, it must be done in the old-fashioned way, which dates back to World War II. Teams of trained people must go out in mobile tracking units and hunt you down while you are transmitting. And if you are moving, this will be next to impossible.

VOICE MAIL

If you can get a voice-mail number (VMN) in a system not tied into your home telephone, by all means do it, preferably using a simple name and an out-of-state address. Use your real number only for close friends and relatives, and the VMN for everyone else. (Voice-mail systems vary not only from state to state but from town to town, so I cannot give you any overall advice. This one you must research on your own.)

Using your voice-mail number: For a library card, give your ghost address and the VMN. When the lady at the used bookstore gives you credit for old books you turn in, and asks for your telephone number, cheerfully give her your VMN. (Unlike at

RadioShack, you will not be asked for your name, nor will the telephone number go into a national database. They just use it in a single computer for identification.) When you take your old Jaguar to the dealer to find that bug in the electrical system, give the service manager your VMN. When you buy that round-trip ticket to the Turks and Caicos Islands, give the travel agent your VMN. But if you go to a clinic for an AIDS test, don't give them any number at all. *You* will call *them*.

PREPAID TELEPHONE CARDS

You've seen them advertised everywhere, but prices vary widely. PostNet and Target stores charge between 19 and 25 cents a minute, and some BP gas stations have a card for 17 cents a minute. (There have been a number of scam operations, selling prepaid cards that do not work, so be sure to purchase only from a legitimate source.) In addition to using them when traveling, use them from home for sensitive calls. Since you must first dial an 800 number, no record will go on your bill, nor will your number show up on Caller ID.

Avoid any card that has this sticker on it:

URGENT! Your card cannot be used until you call us. Call now *from your home phone* to confirm you have received your card [followed by an 800 number].

The issuing company wants you to call from your home telephone so they can capture the number and then sell it to telemarketing companies. Even if there is no sticker, never renew, because you will have to furnish a credit-card number. Buy a new card.

Unfortunately, prepaid phone cards do not work for toll-free destination numbers. (A PI once tried to explain to me why this is so, but I don't think he understood it himself.) If you plan to call a sensitive 800 or 888 number such as to the FBI or IRS, first call from a pay phone or a cellular phone. Tell them a friend wants to call in from Europe and needs a regular number since the 800 doesn't work from overseas. Then, another day, call the regular number from your home, using the calling card.

Important: Even though you are calling a "standard" number (not toll free), if you are making a sensitive call to the local police or to a state or federal agency, do not depend on call blocking. Most of these agencies have the same capabilities as with 911 calls (see below), so *use your prepaid card.*

Do not carry the card itself. If one of these cards is traced back to you, all numbers called from that card can be obtained from the issuing company. Copy the correct 800 number but alter the last two digits. Use the same system for all cards, such as adding or subtracting some easy-to-remember two-digit number. Write this altered number down and then destroy the card. I carry several such numbers in my wallet, jotted down along with other numbers and abbreviated notations that will make no sense to anyone else. For ultra-ultraprivacy, use separate cards for separate sensitive calls, so that if the calls on one card become known, there will be no crossover to the second party.

Warning: Do not fall for the latest phone-card trick being used by PIs. If the private investigator has your mailing address but does not know where you actually live, he or she may mail you a "free phone card." And yes, it will indeed have free minutes— lots of free minutes. Where's the catch? These cards are issued by a company that then furnishes the PI with the number of *every single call you make using that card!*

CALLS TO 911

When you call 911, your true address shows up on the operator's monitor, along with whatever name your telephone is in. If it is listed in another name, will you be able to give a reason for this when the police arrive? (Even if the call was for an ambulance, the police usually arrive first.) To illustrate both the problem and the solution, consider the recent experience we had in a western state.

I was sitting at my computer, making a last-minute revision for this book, when I happened to glance out the window. Here came Walter, one of my neighbors, dragging his big black dog on a leash, racing up to my door. He started pounding on it before I could get there to open it.

"A horse just fell on Julie," he exclaimed, pointing to the east pasture, "and she broke her leg! *Call 9-1-1!*"

At this particular home I unfortunately do have a hard line, used only to receive incoming faxes from a forwarded 800 number, but of course I can call out in an emergency, and Walter knew it. Thoughts raced through my aging brain:

If I call 911 on the hard line, my call blocking will not work. The name the telephone is in (not mine) will show up, and my address as well (the home is not in my name either). They will ask my name and where I live, compare it with the readout on the computer screen, and the conversation will be recorded and filed. While I stood at the door, hesitating not more than a second, Walt spread his hands out and shouted, "JACK, CALL 911!"

I grabbed my cell phone out of its charging unit and called 911.

"*This is 911,*" said a female voice, adding the name of the county.

"I'm calling from a cell phone and—"

"*Yes, I know. What is the emergency?*"

"A lady just had an accident with her horse and broke her leg."

"*Where is the location?*" [I described the general location of the pasture.]

"*How old is this lady?*"

"I don't know, maybe fifty or sixty."

"*Where are you now?*" (I named the road and said I would wait there to direct the emergency vehicle.)

"*What is your name and where do you live?*"

"One moment please, something has just—" and at this point I punched the power off on my cell phone.

I went to the street and was there to direct the emergency vehicle in on the proper lane. A neighbor was already on the scene with a blanket, so I evaporated before any of the crew could ask me if I was the one that called.

Some say that the 911 system may not be able to bring a cell phone name and number onto the screen, but I suspect that in some areas it can. However, even if the number did come up, the only details the telephone company could have provided would have been a common name with no Social Security number, plus a mailing address in another state.

Earlier in this chapter, I discussed the case of a police detective's wife who called 911 and thus revealed their true address. They then had to sell their home and move. But did she have any options? I think so, and you would do well to review these with other members of your family.

1. If they had a cell phone (and they should have!), she could have used that to make the call to 911.

2. Had prior arrangements been set up, she could have called a friend who would in turn call 911 from *her* home, directing the ambulance to such-and-such an address where the detective's wife was *visiting*.

3. When checking in at the hospital, she could have given their ghost address, adding that she was just house-sitting for a friend when the emergency came up.

WATCH OUT FOR THIS SNEAKY TRICK

Suppose a private investigator wants to hear you talking to your lawyer (or mistress, or whoever). He may place a conference call, recording every word. Here is how it works. The first call would go to you, and when you answer, the PI punches HOLD and then speed-dials your lawyer. You start saying "Hello? Hello?" Then your lawyer comes on the line. He recognizes your voice. Each of you may then *assume* the other person placed the call, and start to chat!

Remedy: When a call comes in from a sensitive party, and there is some confusion about who called whom, *ask*. If neither called the other, you have just had a heads-up that someone is after one or both of you.

QUESTIONS & ANSWERS

In the case of a life-or-death situation where neither privacy nor legality matter, what is the fastest way to get help?

Call either the fire department or 911 and report a fire in progress! Captain Robert L. Snow, in his book *Protecting Your Life, Home and Property*, says that if you live in a high crime area and call 911 on a hot summer weekend and/or a busy day, there may be a delay in getting a policeman to your home. He says there have been cases where police dispatchers have listened as a caller was murdered before the police arrived.

Some persons under these circumstances have called the fire department and reported a fire. "This should be done only in desperate situations," says Snow, "since there will likely be some legal consequences later because of calling in a false fire alarm. . . . But if you have absolutely no doubt there is an intruder who knows you're in the home and is trying to get in anyway, there's a very good chance you will be raped, beaten, and/or murdered. At a time like this you can't really worry about legal niceties. There's not much point in being completely law-abiding if you're dead."

How safe are public telephones?

Some of them, especially at the bigger airports and bus terminals, are tapped. There shouldn't be any problem using one at a restaurant or bar, as long as it's not in an area known for prostitution or drug dealing. Pay with coins or use a prepaid calling card. But be careful *whom* you call—the telephone *at the other end* may be tapped.

Sometimes I hear clicking noises on my telephone. I brought in a detective to check for bugs and he said there weren't any, but what if he was wrong? How can I be sure my telephone isn't tapped?

If the government is after you, they will do the tap at a central office and no detective will ever track that one down. In fact, a little test might be to have Detective A install the best tap he knows, and then see if Detective B can find it. (Let me know if you do that; I've got $20 that says Detective B will miss it.) Here is the best advice you'll ever get about telephone security. Have a little label stuck on every telephone that says, THIS LINE IS TAPPED.

Can you recommend a hacker-proof answering machine?

There is no such thing! If I were an electronics engineer, that would be my first project, to invent a secure answering machine. One PI I know with six agents says this is numero uno on his wish list—a number where his agents could call in to leave and pick up messages in absolute secrecy.

The truth—sad to say—is that a number of companies sell answering-machine code breakers that can break into a machine in about ninety seconds. Also, government agents have some interesting equipment, as outlined in *Manhunter*, a book by U.S. Marshal John Pascucci. He was in England, trying to get Scotland Yard to put a tap on a certain producer's phone. They refused.

"After we struck out on the phone tap," says Pascucci, "I called the producer's house to see if he had an answering machine. He did. So I had my computer guys make me a list of all possible three-digit access codes. Finally we hit the right number and started monitoring his messages."

How can I turn off the "redial" feature on my telephone?

You mean, so no one can check your telephone in your absence, to see who you last called? Although this feature cannot be turned off, it can be easily defeated. When you finish your call, hang up. Then pick up the receiver, listen for the dial tone, and punch in a single digit. Then hang up. If anyone checks the "last number called," all they will find is that single digit.

Can international telephone calls be monitored without a warrant?

Of course, because they are beamed by microwave, and there is no law against monitoring microwave transmissions. The National Security Agency (NSA) does this all the time.

I am in serious need of privacy but I also need a monitored burglar alarm, which requires a telephone line. Any suggestions?

For serious privacy, I advocate having no hard-line telephone in your home at all. As for burglar alarms, even if the telephone lines are buried and not easily accessible, crooks can find a way around this. One way is to locate a junction box and cut the service to an entire neighborhood . . . including yours. Alarms are available that connect your alarm system to the monitoring center by radio waves—no way to cut those out. Also, as I said earlier, keep a cell phone close by, in case you need to call the police.

How can I send a fax without having my machine print a heading?

Many stand-alone models do print a heading, and this cannot be turned off. You may wish to set the machine to print an x or a zero for everything. Or, insert an address in a land far, far away. Be sure to set the fax's internal clock to a time zone that will match the foreign address.

If you send faxes from your computer, you should be able to set it so that there is no heading whatsoever. Use the fax machine for receiving only.

Warning: According to the Telephone Consumer Protection Act of 1991, it is unlawful for any person to send a fax unless the fax clearly contains information that includes (1) the date and time it was sent, (2) the name of the person or business sending the fax, and (3) the telephone number of the sending machine.

However, in my opinion as a layman, not a lawyer, the warning can be taken as a very mild one. The above law is violated thousands of times a minute and I have never heard of it ever being enforced. (If any reader knows otherwise, please contact me with the details.)

If I have Caller ID, will it always show the true number of an incoming call?

Usually, but not always. There are hundreds of telephone companies out there, and each operates differently. For example, suppose you live in Los Angeles. Vito, a caller who lives near you, might have a friend in New York temporarily forward his telephone to your number. Then, when Vito calls the New York number and it forwards on to your telephone, your caller screen may show the New York number.

More commonly, you may get false readings when called by any government agency. Although this is supposed to be a secret, Mickey Hawkins, head of the FBI office in Tulsa, Oklahoma, in an interview for an article in the July 5, 1999 *Los Angeles Times*, is quoted as saying, "We use a device that gives a different number."

What wouldn't I give to get my hands on a similar device. . . .

There is, however, one way to indicate you are calling from a location other than your own. The hard part is to find the location; the rest is easy. If you have a faraway friend who'll put in an extra line for you with call forwarding (offer to pay his complete basic phone bill every month), have the phone jack for that line hidden in a closet there. Your friend uses a phone at that phone jack just long enough to forward all calls to your home number, then unplugs it. You will, of course, pay long-distance charges from your friend's home to yours.

What is a "trap line"?

A trap line is a toll-free number used by private investigators to identify the location you are calling from. As soon as the target makes a call, the company providing this service contacts the PI to report the number and location of the incoming call. Remember, since the trap line number starts with either 800 or 888, you cannot block the transmission of information.

If you are the target and the PI has only your mail drop, he may send you a convincing postcard or letter, asking you to either call him or send a fax. If you call or fax from home, he's got you.

Or, perhaps he does not have an address for you but he does have a telephone number for a friend or relative. He will call them while they are away at work, hoping for an answering machine. If there is one, he will leave a message—have so-and-so call me before tomorrow midnight! "Urgent, there is a deadline, can't wait!"

On the other hand, in the case of a dispute between husband and wife, the wife may go to a PI to find out if hubby really is "working late," or "on a business trip." In this case the PI knows his address and home telephone number, but he wants to know where the husband is at the times he is absent. Assume the husband carries a beeper. The wife gives this number to the PI and explains how to mark it *urgent*. During the next suspicious absence, the PI calls the beeper and gives the trap line number. Perhaps the husband was supposed to be on a trip to Sacramento, but the call comes in from the Kit-Kat club north of Reno.

HOW TO FIND AND USE NOMINEES

Panic comes suddenly like thunder from a blue sky. No shrewdness can foresee and no talent avert it.

—MATTHEW SMITH

As you know, an attorney filing a lawsuit may name anyone he pleases. For instance, if he is suing a corporation, he may name the directors, the officers, and even the part-time secretary who writes the checks.

No matter how innocent you are, if you are *named*, you have to defend yourself, and that costs time, money, and extreme aggravation.

So then, if you wish to remain invisible, your name must not surface anywhere. Is that difficult? Yes! But is it impossible? No, but you cannot do this alone. When panic strikes like thunder, you will want a nominee to take the strike!

The dictionary definition of nominee is, "A person named, or designated, by another, to any office, duty, or position; one nominated, or proposed, by others for office or for election to office." As used here, a nominee is someone who will do your bidding like a puppet on a string. (No, don't name your dog J. Pierpont Morgan and use him—the nominee must be able to either sign documents or give oral or written permission to you to sign for him.)

Further information about running a low-profile business—or even one that is invisible—will be covered in Chapter 15. What will be discussed here is the selection of a nominee.

A nominee is someone you "nominate" to take your place. This could be another person who takes your place as the apparent owner or manager of a company you own. More often, it will be a person who—on your behalf—opens a bank account, obtains a cellular telephone, or signs up for your utilities.

Who might be an ideal candidate? You may already have someone in mind, but if not, here are a few suggestions:

- A homeless person who has not filed a tax return since Truman beat Dewey.
- That illegal Guatemalan whom a friend hired to take care of the kids.
- The town drunk, who sobers up just long enough to sign some "papers" in return for a case of Thunderbird.
- A relative or close friend who will do this as a favor.
- Someone who owes you money, is not in a position to pay you back, and would act as nominee in return for clearing the loan.

On the other hand, here is who *not* to use:

- Do not use a lover or a mistress—when the affair goes sour, he or she will see you drawn and quartered!
- Do not use an unwilling candidate. Example: "Look, Bill, either I name you as a member and you give me a notarized power of attorney, or I'll tell your parents about the time the police nailed you in that XXX movie place."

This is blackmail.

Whatever the case, you should choose someone who has no assets, otherwise known as "judgment-proof." Then, when a lawyer discovers there are no assets to recover, no lawsuit will be filed.

Age: From time to time I do use a young person, especially if from Spain or Mexico. However, all else being equal, older is better and *really* old is best. There are several problems involved in using young persons.

For one thing, although broke now, they may get their ducks in a row and start making money. Or they might inherit money when their parents or grandparents die. Or they might be injured in an accident and receive tens of thousands of dollars in compensation. At that point, they would *not* be judgment-proof.

QUESTIONS & ANSWERS

Is a nominee something I should consider, even though I am not in business?

Yes, of course. A nominee can help you make a smooth transition to privacy. Imagine, for example, that you decide to move to another location, even if close by. You ask your aunt Bertha from Presque Isle, Maine, to travel to your area and help out. Here is what she can do:

- Sign the new lease.
- Get all utilities in her name.
- Order normal telephones, a cell phone, and a pager.
- Get a ghost address that is to serve for both you and her. (It will actually be yours only.)

Where required, a deposit will be paid rather than giving a Social Security number. Have her open a new account and turn the account over to you. From this point forward you will send all deposits by mail.

If you die before she does, she will own the account. But that's fair, is it not? However, if you are worried about *her* untimely death, then using her as the sole member of a limited-liability company may solve any complications that otherwise might arise in such a case, as she could leave the membership to you in her will. (See Chapter 12.)

10

USING A TRUST FOR PRIVACY

To have is nothing. To keep is all.

—UNKNOWN

Before writing about trusts I searched the Internet for any reference whatsoever to forming a revocable trust (or "living trust") solely for purposes of privacy. Thousands of references to revocable trusts (*inter vivos*) scrolled across my computer, brought up by Magellan, Yahoo!, AltaVista, Excite, Elnet Galaxy, InfoSeek, WebCrawler, and Lycos. I can and do read small print rapidly, but after three hours and forty-two minutes I called it quits.

Unless my skills at Boolean searches need an update, not one attorney out there in cyberspace discusses privacy as the *principal* reason for the formation of a revocable trust. (By revocable I mean you can change your mind and cancel the whole deal.)

Abandoning the Net, I next rechecked the indexes of those rare books in my library that happen to have an index. One book on asset protection does have an index and it does list two references under the word "Privacy." The first reference doesn't apply to secret ownership of assets within the United States, however, and the other, on page 117, merely says, "Deploy your assets and investments in a way that requires the least amount of detailed information on your tax returns."

So I, a nonlawyer, am on my own here. If you already understand terms like grantor, trustor, settlor, trustee, and beneficiary, you may wish to skip the information that follows. Otherwise, if your knowledge about trusts is a little fuzzy, then perhaps the following will help. But, remember, all I can provide is my best understanding as a layman, which is no substitute for professional legal advice.

WHAT IS A TRUST?

A living trust is a legal document that resembles a will. It contains your instructions for the distribution of the your assets when you die. By "assets," I refer to your home, vehicles, bank accounts, stocks and bonds, copyrights, and so on. Trusts can be broadly categorized as either testamentary trusts or living (*inter vivos*) trusts. A testamentary trust is created within a will and takes effect only at death. A living trust is a trust that you create during your lifetime, and that is what we are discussing here. Besides keeping your affairs private during your lifetime, if all your assets are in a living trust when you die, you completely avoid probate and thus your privacy extends beyond the grave.

The reason that a trust is so private is that it is never recorded with any county, city, state, or federal authority. There is a document in your lawyer's office and one for your files. That's it.

Think of a trust as a holding pen, a place where you put your assets before they are released—after death—to the people or organizations that you designate. Because you and the trust are separate legal entities, anything you transfer from you to the trust becomes property of the trust. The trust then holds the property for your benefit, or for the benefit of those whom you designate. It consists of four components:

- The grantor, who creates the trust. That's you and/or your wife.
- The beneficiaries, who will eventually receive the assets. This is often your spouse, and after the death of your spouse, your children.
- The assets, which are the properties transferred to the trust.
- The trustee, who is the person or entity that manages the trust's assets and distributes the property according to terms established by the grantor. Even though you are the grantor, you can also be the trustee, and thus be in charge of all assets in the trust. When you die, of course, someone else must take charge, in order to pass the assets on to the beneficiaries.

The trust here being discussed is a *revocable* trust, which means you can change it at any time.

HOW A REVOCABLE TRUST IS FORMED

Let's say your name is Grant and you wish to prepare a document ("trust") that will hold property just as if it were in your own name. First, make a rough draft on your own, based on what you hope to accomplish. Then, take it to your lawyer for review. (Call him "counselor" or refer to him as your "attorney," since lawyers dislike the word "lawyer.")

Tell him or her you want a simple, revocable trust solely for privacy, both a short form and a long form, and would he please look over your rough draft? (You don't need a draft, of course, but you save money by not having him start from scratch.) He asks you a few questions. (I just named you "Grant Settler" and gave you a wife, "Trudy.")

Grant, who's going to form this, you and your wife?
"Yes, Trudy and me."
And if both of you should die, who will get whatever the trust owns?
"My niece Benita Ficiary."
Who will be in charge of putting things into the trust, and taking things out?
"Me and Trudy, is that OK?"
That's fine. And should you both die, who should then take charge of the trust?
"Um, let's put Gordon Goodfriend."
And if Gordon dies?
"Well, put, uh, let's see. Mary Secondcousin." (In the unlikely event that *all* the beneficiaries die, the assets would then pass into the estate.)
No problema. I'll have it ready Tuesday. A hundred fifty will cover it. Oh say, we need a name. How about "Settler Family Trust"? (Does this lawyer have a room-temperature IQ?)
"No, do not, repeat, NOT, use my name. Let's name it after Trudy's late great-grandfather and call it the *Wladyslaw Truszowsky Family Trust.*" (You reach for a pen to write out the name.)
Listen, Grant, maybe there's someone still alive somewhere with that name, and there's a chance this could cause you trouble. (Oh-oh, the attorney now earns a brownie point.) *Where were you born, Trudy?*
"On a farm," says Trudy, "north of Moonshine Junction, Montana. But the general store burned down in 1952 and now the town doesn't exist anymore."
All the better! Let's call this the "Moonshine Junction Trust."
"Yeah, that has a nice ring to it," you answer. "See you Tuesday then, counselor. Have a good day."

The lawyer will give you both a short-term and a long-term form of the trust. The long form is to keep in your files. The short form, with less information, is what you will present (when asked) to your bank, at the Motor Vehicles Department, at the title company, or wherever. The purpose for this is to prove that you are a trustee and have the authority to sign on your own.

DO NOT *ASSUME* ANYTHING

"Do not assume anything," I tell my clients, "when you put a title into a trust." That's what I tell others and that's what I generally practice, but last year I was caught. A certain "leading lawyer" in a Western city was to act on my behalf in the purchase of some rural acreage. I clearly explained my viewpoint on privacy and that the title deed must be in the name of my trust *only*. The actual cotrustee (me) was not to be listed. (Sometimes I get by with this, sometimes not—but if not, I expected him to call me for instructions.)

Nevertheless when the title was recorded, it appeared my name was listed as trustee. I flew in to this city and went straight to the county courthouse, where I asked the clerk in the assessor's office to check the property list on her computer for anything owned by a "J. J. Luna." Ten seconds later my name was on the screen: *J. J. Luna, trustee, R—Trust!*

When I stormed into the lawyer's office I got stonewalled— he said it certainly wasn't *his* fault, he "*had* to list the trustee, everybody knows that!" If I wanted the land retitled, I'd have to pay him at his usual hourly rate. *Hah!*

Here is what any dimwit so-called lawyer not more than two tacos short of a combo plate would have done, if told at the courthouse that they had to list a trustee:

1. He would mumble something about incomplete data and *retreat*.

2. He would then call me with these suggestions:

(a) Allow him to list the alternate trustee (in this case my wife, using her maiden name), or

(b) Suggest I get a *new* cotrustee and list that one, or

(c) Have him title the land with one of my other legal entities, or

(d) Furnish the name of a temporary nominee—perhaps himself.

3. Until he had my answer, he would have done *nothing*.

The only reason I do not list this lawyer's name is that although I transferred the land into another name (on my own), he knows the location and thus the details. But other than with this poor excuse for a lawyer, I've had no problem with any of our trusts.

A REVOCABLE TRUST IS NOT COMPLICATED

Don't let lawyers or authors confuse you with obscure terms. A revocable trust, when formed mainly for purposes of privacy, is simple. If your lawyer confuses you and tells you never mind the details, you may wish to change lawyers. Points to remember:

- Although not a do-it-yourself project, this is not, or should not be, expensive. Maybe $250 tops.

- There are no annual fees.

- There is no record other than the "short form" copies you choose to give to your bank, the DMV, or a title company.

- You can revoke (cancel) the trust at any time.

- It does not affect your tax return; you treat the asset as your own.

- There are ancillary benefits in case of death, which your lawyer will explain.

There is of course no asset protection with a revocable trust, nor are there any tax savings, but we are here discussing *privacy* only.

If you want protection and savings added in, then we'll fast-forward to my absolute favorite kind of irrevocable (unchangeable) trust.

THE CHARITABLE REMAINDER UNITRUST

Although little known just five years ago, this unique entity's fifteen minutes of fame is fast approaching. Unlike the assets in a revocable trust, once you make a donation to a charitable remainder unitrust the assets are beyond the reach of anyone. If you are sued and a judgment is filed against you, or even if you file for bankruptcy, the assets cannot be touched because this is an *irrevocable* trust—you can never change it. You'll get tax-free capital gains (if applicable) and a huge tax deduction. The trust will earn tax-free income and will pay you a high rate of interest for as long as you (and a surviving mate, if any) live.

Although setting up a charitable remainder unitrust is not a do-it-yourself project, if you have highly appreciated assets, the legal fee, which may be about $3,000, is worth it. (See Chapter 15, the mail-order business from Nevada.) Just be sure you use an experienced lawyer who has *already* set up many such trusts. For the annual tax returns (no tax is ever due), find a CPA who has references from others who have similar trusts. It is vital that the calculation of the annual amount withdrawn is correct.

QUESTIONS & ANSWERS

What about "common law" trusts—are they for real?

I am sometimes asked about "constitutional" or "common law" trusts. Some think that they can legally avoid paying income taxes by using these trusts, and cite various United States Supreme Court decisions in support of their position. There is no legal foundation for any such claims. About three years ago, an article in the *Colorado Lawyer* reported that the IRS was conducting a nationwide program to examine these trusts. Not a good sign, folks. Forget about common law trusts.

What about "unorganized business trusts"?

The infamous UBTs? Same answer.

11

STRANGE USES FOR CORPORATIONS

Don't ask the barber whether you need a haircut.

—FIRST LAW OF EXPERT ADVICE

Do not ask a lawyer whether you need a corporation, nor take the advice in just any book. You could spend $10,000 on books about corporations and incorporating, and take three months off work to study the laws of the fifty states and the District of Columbia. At the end of that time you might be even more confused than you were at the beginning, so here is how I'm going to cover the subject of corporations in this chapter:

First, I'll define what a corporation is, in the simplest way I can (*over*simplified where necessary), just to be sure you have the general idea of what a corporation is, and isn't. *I will discuss the standard or "C" corporation only because with the advent of limited-liability companies, "S" corporations are en route to the morgue.*

Second, I'll cite examples where even the "experts" display their ignorance. This will encourage you to press on, learn this section by heart, and at the next cocktail party you can maybe even tell an F. Lee Bailey–type of lawyer a thing or two about the very best states in America for *privacy*.

Third, I'll explain how I myself have used corporations to accomplish what otherwise couldn't have been legally done, and then I'll cite examples of how others have been able to attain specific goals via corporations and limited-liability companies.

Fourth, I'll discuss which state is the best for incorporating, and review my reasons for not recommending Delaware or Nevada.

Fifth and final: The moment of decision! By this time you'll have decided if I've walked the walk or just talked the talk. If the former, then you'll want to pay attention to what follows.

Note: Much of what I say about corporations could also apply to limited-liability companies (called LLCs—see Chapter 12). Just keep in mind that both of these legal entities are like the puppet I am about to describe. Think of a corporation as a brother whose twin fraternal sister is an LLC. Both persons are very similar, same family, same traits. It's just that under certain circumstances the anatomical differences must be considered.

OK, fasten your seat belt and let's roll.

WHAT IS A CORPORATION?

A corporation is like a legal person who is born in a specific place, called a domicile. The domicile is the state where the corporation was registered. For example, if you form a corporation in Illinois, you can do business with it in Florida. However, you will register it there as a "foreign" corporation because the domicile does not change. It remains in Illinois.

A director is appointed and this director can tell this legal person what to do. In other words, the corporation is like a mindless puppet, and thus needs a director to pull the strings. The puppet can be owned by other persons, or by other legal entities, or by the director. (If it is not owned by one director, then the owners—called shareholders—can fire the director and hire another one to pull the strings.)

This puppet can do most anything you can, and often—as we'll see—it can do things that you cannot. Further, if someone tries to bomb you back to the Stone Age it's the puppet that gets zipped into a body bag. Or, if someone sues and gets a judgment for $500,000, the only money at risk is what's in the puppet's pocket. Your private assets are safe. We are talking serious privacy here.

The above assumes you have capitalized your corporation with a reasonable amount of money, kept proper books and minutes, and have not mingled your own funds in with the company. Otherwise, in legalese, you may be accused of undercapitalization, and/or maintaining the company as your alter ego. Should such be the case, someone suing you might thus be able to "pierce the corporate veil."

This is one area where a limited-liability company has a huge advantage over the corporation, since *bookwork and protocol are far simpler with an LLC.*

"EXPERTS" DISPLAY THEIR IGNORANCE

I've met a few good lawyers in the Canary Islands and many bad ones, which parallels my experiences with American attorneys. The U.S. has the *most* competent attorneys working side by side with the *least* competent, and the latter outnumber the former 666 to 1. In fact, given a choice between the most competent paralegal and the least competent lawyer, I'll take the paralegal in a heartbeat, so let's have a little chat about U.S. lawyers, along with other experts real or imagined.

In 1988, I flew from the Canaries to Nevada to set up two corporations in that state. [I no longer recommend Nevada, but at that time it was satisfactory.] In Carson City I met with one of the city's leading attorneys to have his office act as the resident agent, rather than going through one of the "incorporation mills."

In the course of a low-cost lunch at the Carson Nugget Casino, I asked this lawyer if he'd kindly name a few of the more unusual uses for the many Nevada corporations he'd formed over a long lifetime. That is, uses other than the ones in all the books. (Liability protection, tax savings, prestige, continuity, etc.) Well . . . this lawyer couldn't think of *any* unusual uses, not one! I won't name him here because I've since put this same question to other American lawyers and they pretty much don't have any original ideas either! In fact, a year ago I asked an old-time corporate attorney in Albuquerque (licensed also in Utah, Wyoming, and New York) how many clients he'd had over the years who formed a corporation specifically for the purpose of privacy.

"Uh, I guess maybe . . . um . . . none."

"None at *all?*" I said. "I can scarcely believe it."

"Well, maybe it was my fault," he admitted. "To tell the truth, I never thought about it, never gave anyone a chance. Just told 'em they *had* to list this, list that, put down everything . . ."

Guess which attorney I didn't use in Albuquerque? But let's not leave out experts and accountants. An astronomical number of accountants—especially CPAs—know far less about corporations than they claim to know, and few authors come out well when they write about incorporating. Here is a recent example.

My good friends Pat and Patty Lindquist, who build houses under their own name, asked me to recommend a good beginner's guidebook to teach them about corporations in general. I said I'd pick one up. A few weeks later I happened to be staying at the Waterfront Plaza Hotel in Oakland, on Jack London Square. I had some free time so I walked across the square to the Barnes & Noble bookstore there, to check out the business section. The best of the worst, on the subject of incorporating, was a well-known book by a recognized author.

I bought this book, the newest ninth edition, but before I gave it to my friends, I flipped through it. On page 22, it reads, "All corporations must have a word like Company, Corporation, Incorporated, or their abbreviations in their titles." I have personally formed forty-seven corporations in the United States with none of those words at the end. It can still be done in this current year. As for other advice, on page 39, the author says that both savings and checking accounts "require the impression of your corporate seal." This is simply not so—ask any banker. Also, on the same page, the author says, "Start your corporate checks with high numbers, like 626 or 340. It makes your corporation look like it's been established for years."

For *years?* With a three-digit number like 626 or 340? I currently start all my company bank accounts with at least a high four-digit number and often with 15,001 or higher. This is an easy way to "age" your company.

On page 45, referring to limited-liability companies, the author says, "LLCs require at least two members . . . so if you are a single entrepreneur or professional, you may wish to form an S corporation instead." *Many* states allow one-member LLCs, and S corporations [a tax option where corporate income flows through to the owners] are dying.

Nevertheless, I do not mean to put the author down. On the contrary, if all you want is an introduction to the garden-variety uses of corporations, then I recommend the book. I merely add this caveat: skip her comments on check numbers, corporate seals, and LLCs.

Speaking of LLCs, be very cautious about getting information on these companies from just any lawyer. Why do I say this? Because of bad experiences with lawyers who hold themselves out to be experts in a certain field, and yet lack crucial knowledge in that very field! A personal experience will serve as an example:

Four years ago, I needed to clarify a point of marine law before forming an LLC that would take ownership of a small yacht. It was to be based in Point Roberts, Washington, which sits on a little tip of land jutting into Puget Sound from British Columbia. I therefore made some calls to legal organizations in the Seattle area, asking for the *absolute expert* in marine law in the Northwest. It was agreed that my man was a certain attorney near the Canadian border. I called this lawyer to discuss what I planned to do, but at the instant I said ownership would be taken with a limited-liability company he interrupted me.

"You mean a corporation."

"No," I said, "it has to be an LLC."

"Same thing as a corporation."

When I tried to correct him, did he admit he might be a wee tad behind the times? No! He *insisted* that there was positively no such thing in the state of Washington. The next day I made a copy of the Washington LLC statutes that I had in my files (they took effect October 1, 1994) and sent this to him by priority mail, asking for his comments. No answer was ever forthcoming, nor is one expected—one class you will not find in many law schools is *Common Courtesy 101*.

UNUSUAL USES FOR CORPORATIONS

There are many uses for corporations and LLCs that your lawyer has never heard of, but which may spark an idea of your own. The two examples that follow are culled from my clients in Europe who use American corporations and LLC for various reasons—usually privacy. Over the years, I formed more than 1400 U.S. legal entities for them and the principals involved apply equally well for those of you who live in the United States. If any of the true experiences that follow inspire you to come up with your own unusual use, please let me know. I may incorporate your idea in the next edition of this book.

First, allow me to explain the difference between United States and European corporations. In the U.S., corporations are tied not just to the country but to an individual state or the District of Columbia, thus giving you a choice of fifty-one different sets of statutes and regulations. Not so in continental Europe, where there's but one choice per country, none of which is appetizing. Often, $10,000 or more has to be posted permanently as a cash bond, and getting the right kind of name may be impossible. There are literally thousands of names acceptable ·

in the United States that are *verboten* overseas, and as you read along in this section, I urge you to think not only about unusual uses, but unusual corporate names as well.

Can't get no respect

My client Lazlo K. from Budapest started purchasing some sort of product from Russia (I didn't ask for details) and exporting it in containers. One container was shipped to Mombasa, Kenya, on the east coast of Africa.

The port authorities wanted a large bribe to get the container released, higher than the Hungarian was willing to pay. The container therefore sat on the dock for five long months. There was no political solution, as Hungary gets *no* respect in the international world of commerce. Finally, in desperation, the bribe was paid. This wiped out most of the profit on the shipment, and there was more bad news—with the original order, Lazlo had committed himself to sending two more containers to Kenya! Can this story have a happy ending?

Yes, but only because I formed in the United States, on his behalf, the *New York International Container and Air Freight Corporation*, with Lazlo as sole director. He then shipped the next two containers, not in his own name, but in the name of the New York International Container and Air Freight Corporation.

The two containers arrived in Mombasa, Kenya, and the Hungarian flew in a day later. This time his first visit was not to the port area but to the American consulate. He presented his shipping papers, identified himself as the director of the New York International Container and Air Freight Corporation and explained some previous problems he had had with port authorities. The American consul made just one phone call on his behalf, and the containers were off the dock within forty-eight hours.

Lesson to be learned: If you, like Rodney Dangerfield, "can't get no respect" in the business world, consider an upscale name. (The example just mentioned would have worked equally well as a limited-liability company.)

PRESTIGE

When conversation among friends starts to drag, I sometimes pep it up with this, the strangest corporate-name case I've come across so far. Here's the story: At the end of February 1992 I received a faxed order from Achim Eckel, a client in Germany who had previously purchased several U.S. corporations. In his previous orders he'd used routine German-language names with "A.G." as the corporate identifier, but this time was different. The name section of the order blank was filled in with five words, as follows:

EUROPEAN BANCORP DOCTOR ACHIM ECKEL

I thought an error had been made in this last order, so I faxed Eckel back for confirmation. Did he perhaps mean the corporate name was EUROPEAN BANCORP, but he, Dr. Achim Eckel, was to be listed as director? Or perhaps some punctuation was missing? Back came the answer: *Form the corporation as shown. No punctuation. No listed director.*

OK, no problem, even though I failed to understand the logic behind the name. (Looking back, I wonder how I missed it.) Later on, I got the story from a man who knew my client well, but first, some brief background about Germany and Germans. The basic laws that existed in Adolf Hitler's Germany are still the laws of Germany today—most of the laws *did not change* after World War II. And one of Hitler's laws, passed in the 1930s, was that no German could call himself a doctor unless he *was* a doctor. If he did, the penalty for the first offense was *one year in jail.* Therefore, no German would ever call himself a doctor without the proper degree, right? Uh, not necessarily.

It may be difficult, if you are American-born, to understand the German craving for a title, but for some Germans it is an obsession. In fact, I've earned enough to pay for a few semesters at the University of Heidelberg by forming corporations with the word "University" in the name. The German client then gives himself a work contract and prints up new business cards with PROFESSOR before his name!

The absolute best title, however, is doctor, and if a German is a doctor, I never fail to address him as such. Even there, I was caught off base once. A fax came in from Berlin with some urgent questions about bearer shares. It was from a Doctor Doctor Klein, someone new. I hurriedly answered his questions, addressing him, of course, as Dr. Klein, as I thought the second "doctor" was a typo. Big mistake. Back came a fax within a minute. Message:

"Sir, I am not Doctor Klein. I am Doctor *Doctor* Klein!"

He claimed to have titles in *two* fields, and thus must be properly addressed as "Doctor Doctor." That was the way I addressed him in all future faxes, although I've privately wondered if he might not be a candidate for *two* years in a German jail—one year for each "doctor."

Now, after hearing more about the German psyche than you wanted to know, we return to the strange case of the EUROPEAN BANCORP DOCTOR ACHIM ECKEL corporation. As I learned later, Achim Eckel never was and never would be a doctor. Nor did he wish to call himself a doctor and run the very real risk of a year in jail. The U.S. corporation solved his problem. He sits in his office in Berlin. The telephone rings and he picks up the receiver. Notice the accent and the pause when he identifies his business:

"EUROPEAN *BANC*ORP!" [pause]. "Dr. Achim *Eck*el!"

Would you not then address him as Doctor Eckel? Of course you would, and—not knowing the history—so would I. Happily, there is no law in Germany to condemn Eckel if it is only *other* persons who call him a doctor.

Lesson to be learned: Would you like to be called "Judge"? Or "King," or "President for-life"? Now you know one way to go about it.

DELAWARE AND NEVADA CORPORATIONS

As you know, ads have been running for decades advertising low-cost incorporation in Delaware and, to a lesser extent, in Nevada. Hundreds of thousands of corporations have been domiciled in these two states, many for as little as "$19 plus costs." For this reason alone I dislike these two states. Yes, I know that many huge corporations are based in one of these two states, but the usual implication is that anything from Delaware or Nevada is some sort of Mickey Mouse operation. Just ask any judge, private investigator, or courthouse clerk.

Delaware has an income tax, so if you plan to accept income in the state of domicile, Delaware is out. True, Nevada has no corporate income tax as this is written, but they have been quietly raising fees for years, and now have both a franchise and an employee tax. Some Nevada incorporators claim that Nevada is the only state that does not give information to the IRS. Of course they don't. Nevada does not have a state income tax, so what would there be to report? Neither do Alaska, Florida, Wyoming, South Dakota, New Hampshire, or Texas.

For privacy and—in some cases, tax savings—Wyoming is presently the state of choice for a corporation. Directors need not be listed in the articles of incorporation and, unlike Delaware and Nevada, Wyoming does not require a corporate identifier. As has been previously mentioned, you can name your corporation (for example) "Johnny Johnson" [no "Inc."] and no one will know this is a corporation unless you choose to tell them.

Now then, let's talk about money. Are Delaware and Nevada *really* "low-cost"? Certainly not Nevada. Many incorporators fail to mention the additional fee for the Nevada state form for listing directors. Some do not mention the franchise fee. One prominent Nevada incorporator does a brutal hard sell for an "office plan" (i.e., an address and telephone number for the corporation in Carson City). The cost for a two-year contract is $250 per month. Then, when the customer realizes he doesn't need or want that, and stops paying, he is promptly sued via their in-house lawyer!

According to one of my clients in Livermore, California, the post office has on occasion refused to deliver mail to corporations with Nevada addresses unless the company files a special form identifying every corporate officer with his or her home address. Further, the Nevada state offices now have a 900 number for tracking down the names of corporate officers. The cost is just $3.50.

As for Delaware, advertised low costs include neither a corporate kit nor other extras, and the companies make money in the long run by charging high annual fees for the required resident agent.

If you are going to incorporate at all, and if you plan to do business with the corporation in your home state, then the logical choice may be to incorporate in the state where you live. This is because, if you use an out-of-state corporation in your home state *and* wish to have liability protection, you will need to register that corporation in your own state anyway. Thus, you will be paying annual fees to two states.

However, I know of only two unusually good reasons to use a corporation rather than a limited-liability company. One is for the tax savings and perks (such as a medical plan) available with a C corporation ("C" is an option with the IRS where the corporation is taxed separately), and the other is to use a name with no ending (Inc., LLC, etc.) to reveal that it is a legal entity rather than a real person. This latter option is not available to limited-liability companies. They must end in LC or LLC, or similar.

Otherwise, for purposes of privacy, flexibility, and minimum bookkeeping, I strongly recommend a limited-liability company.

12

LIMITED-LIABILITY
COMPANIES (LLCs)

It may take some searching, but there's a lid for every pot.

—Anonymous

Mary L——was a schoolteacher who lived with her husband and four children near Seattle, Washington. In the early 1990s, Mary purchased a gray Volkswagen Fox. In all innocence, she titled the car in her own name. Not in her wildest dreams—or nightmares!—could Mary have foreseen the bitter consequences of driving a car with plates that would show up in the computer with her first name, middle initial, and last name.

Years passed. Unexpectedly, Mary fell in love with one of her students, a thirteen-year-old boy. Despite being married, she was unable to control her emotions. One thing led to another and Mary found herself pregnant. In 1997, the affair became known. She was arrested, jailed, and sentenced to eighty-nine months in prison. Given her lack of a criminal record and the fact she posed no threat to society, Mary was released on parole. One of the conditions of the parole was that she would not contact her young lover without permission from the authorities.

Mary carried a pager. The father of her future child, unable— or unwilling—to stay away from Mary, sent her a page with the number of a pay phone. She called him back. That same evening she picked him up in her little gray Volkswagen Fox.

They went to a late movie, *Wag the Dog*. Then Mary parked her Volkswagen along a street near her home and they talked into the early-morning hours. Mary had already packed and had hidden money and her passport in the car. They apparently made plans to flee Seattle together and to make a new life far, far away.

At that point, was there any obstacle to their plans? The parole board had no idea that Mary was violating parole. She was not wanted by the police. No one else knew of their plans to flee. Nor was society in danger.

[Imagine background music to the movie *Jaws*.]

At 2:45 A.M., Seattle policeman Todd Harris was on a routine patrol. He passed a car that was parked along the curb. The parking lights were on. The windows were steamed up, but it appeared there were two occupants.

There was no sign of misbehavior. Nevertheless, Harris noted the Washington license plate number as he drove by. As he continued on his patrol, he ran the number through his computer to make sure the car had not been reported stolen. Several blocks later the name of the registered owner came onto the screen. The car was legally registered and was not stolen, but he recognized the name from reading about the case in the newspapers.

Mary K. LeTourneau.

Officer Harris returned, and asked for ID. The two occupants were Mary and the boy.

The boy was taken home. Mary was taken to the station, then arrested for violation of parole. On Friday, February 6, 1998, the judge revoked her parole and sentenced her to serve the full eighty-nine months. Leaving aside the morality of meeting with the father of her child, here is the lesson I want you to draw from this story: *At the time Mary titled the car*, there was not—could not have been—the slightest indication of the troubles that lay ahead. But who among us can guarantee that quiet waters will never see a storm? (See my own experiences in Chapter 13.)

After the LeTourneau sentencing, I sent a notice to all my clients in the United States and Canada with this headline:

SEVEN YEARS IN JAIL FOR NOT
USING A LIMITED LIABILITY COMPANY!

You will often hear that a limited-liability company is something "new," but this refers only to the United States. In Europe, LLCs have been used for more than a century and, as mentioned previously, I myself formed my first one in Spain in 1972. As I said in Chapter 10, "Think of a corporation as a brother whose twin fraternal sister is an LLC. Both persons are very similar, same family, same traits. It's just that under certain circumstances the anatomical differences must be considered." So then, let's discuss anatomical differences as applied strictly to limited-liability companies.

Think of an LLC primarily as a partnership, but without the liability and (now hear this!) without the necessity of actually having a partner. It also resembles a corporation but without many of the onerous bookkeeping details and annual meetings.

I've gone over the LLC statutes in virtually every state, and by no means are they all the same. California, Illinois, and New York have outrageously high fees and are not recommended except in the most dire circumstances. Neither are any of the well-known states used for incorporation—the LLC laws are entirely different. I have discovered several states that—although unsuitable for incorporating, are ideal for LLCs, because the *only* information required in the Articles of Organization is:

1. The name of the company,

2. The name and address of the resident agent (to be explained shortly), and

3. The duration of the LLC.

These states do not require the names of members or managers. (Managers, in any case, are not recommended.) The principal office can be anywhere in the world, and a street address is not needed. There need be no mention of capitalization, whether one dollar or a billion.

Further, only a single member is required, not two—as is the case in so many states, and there are *no annual reports*. Thus, changes in membership take place in total darkness. *Neither are there any annual fees*. Compare this with California's annual $800 *(minimum)* franchise tax!

WHICH STATE, AND WHAT WILL IT COST?

At this writing, the state I use for all LLCs—both my own and for my clients—is New Mexico. If you use a lawyer to form the company, figure the cost to vary between $1,500 and $3,000, assuming the lawyer will do it at all. Many will not, as they do not feel qualified to answer your questions and draft a proper operating agreement. An attorney from Florida sent me a video offering his services in setting up limited-liability companies, and quoted a price of $2,000, which is about average. However, he calls them Limited Liability "Corporations," which makes me wonder about his competence in this field.

RESIDENT AGENTS

The laws in all states require that both corporations and limited-liability companies have a resident agent *in that state* who can receive official communications and send them on promptly to the owner or manager of the company. This must be a real street address, not a mail-receiving agency. (If the resident agent resigns—perhaps for nonpayment of his annual fee—then a new resident agent must be found within a short time. If not, the state will dissolve the company.)

Lawyers can form LLCs in any state because they use one of two national resident-agent companies, either CT Corporation or Network (formerly Prentice Hall). Both companies charge attorneys $120 plus fees and costs to file Articles of Organization, plus $165 per year to act as resident agents.

However, in the appendix at the back of this book, I list the address of a young lady in the Canary Islands who charges only $99 to form a New Mexico LLC, and only $99 per year for the resident agent. She has organized or incorporated more that 1,700 corporations and LLCs for me over the past 12 years and is totally, completely reliable.

At first, many of my clients seem confused when I tell them about limited-liability companies. I understand this. When LLCs first started to be used in the U.S., many lawyers were confused. But for the purposes of *privacy*, the use of an LLC can be remarkably simple. When formed correctly, here are the two pages you will receive:

1. CERTIFICATE OF ORGANIZATION

   This official-appearing document with the state seal, signed by both the chairman and the director of the State Corporation Commission, contains this information:

   • Name of the LLC
   • Official number in the state records
   • The effective starting date

   No one has ever asked me for this document. Either frame it and hang it on your office wall, or file it.

2. ARTICLES OF ORGANIZATION
   This is the working document. It contains the following information, all of which is of public record. The organizer (which may or may not be a lawyer) prepares these articles, and often lists a manager, members, true addresses, and other information which is *not* required by the state. However, the organizer referred to above is privacy-

oriented and will include only the following information in the Articles of Organization:

- The name of the LLC.
- The latest date upon which the company is to dissolve (usually fifty years in advance).
- The street address of the company's initial registered office and the name and street address of the company's resident agent. [Both addresses will be the same, that of your agent in the state capital.]
- The address of the company's principal place of business. [This is not a requirement in New Mexico, but a good organizer includes it for an extremely important reason. You must list any address in the world *other than* the state where the LLC is registered because otherwise, it will be assumed to be an in-state company and thus subject to NM state employment laws, with forms to be filed.]

Make copies of the Articles of Organization and have them ready to present when registering your new car, plane, boat, travel trailer, or snowmobile. (See Chapter 13 for detailed, step-by-step instructions.)

HOLDING A COPYRIGHT WITH AN LLC

There are unusual advantages to holding a copyright for a song, play, book, or work of art in the name of an LLC. Remember:

- The LLC name need not show up on any tax return. The income is listed on your personal tax return. No K-2 forms are required if there are no partners.
- If you wish to transfer future income to anyone else, merely transfer ownership of the LLC. (Just a simple letter for the "files" should be sufficient.)

• If you wish to bring the income into a corporation or any other legal entity, merely transfer the ownership.

If you wish to pass ownership on to your children, leave your sole membership to them in your will.

SELLING OR TRANSFERRING OWNERSHIP
OF YOUR LLC

This is where an LLC really shines, especially if you live in a state with a sales tax. Remember, the Articles of Organization *do not name the owner*. If ever there was a case where possession was nine-tenths of the law, possession of the Articles of Organization is it. The LLC is owned by whoever you say owns it—who can prove different? The state does not know. The organizer does not know. *No one* knows unless you tell them! No shares are transferred because an LLC does not have shares. No report is ever made to the state on transfers because there is no annual report.

An obvious question is, "What if someone does not believe you?" I can only say that in nearly thirty years of using LLCs, I have never been asked to prove that I owned one, nor has any client to my knowledge. However, if such a question ever came up, I might offer to prepare and have notarized a statement that I am the sole member (assuming that to be the case). Or, more likely, I would pick a nominee and hand him the LLC, telling him he was "Owner for a Day." To avoid any future question about this, I would draft a simple letter for the files to show the ownership was then transferred back to me. We would both sign. However, there is almost no chance such a situation will ever come up. In this respect, having the Articles of Organization in your hand is similar to having a check in your hand that is made out to "Cash."

If you have multiple legal entities such as corporations, trusts, and other LLCs, do you see how easy it is to transfer ownership? If you buy a new pickup and later transfer it to a company you own, you take the Articles out of your personal file and drop them into the company file. Later, if you decide it would be better to have your trust own it, you switch the Articles to the trust file. If your brother-in-law wants to buy the pickup later, you hand him the Articles and take the cash. Here are the only changes that need be made:

1. Insurance company: Change the insurance to the new owner. This is done by listing the new owner's name, followed by dba ("doing business as") and then the name of the LLC. Example: *John Breadwinner, dba, California Dreamer LLC.*

2. Department of Motor Vehicles: change of address (for receiving the annual registration notice).

Although a pickup is being used as an example, the same principles apply to real estate, boats, loans, options, or whatever. In summary:

1. The article is purchased, received, or acquired in the name of an LLC.

2. Whoever owns the LLC owns the article.

3. Ownership is transferred by handing (or mailing) the LLC to the new owner, along with a letter acknowledging that fact.

4. There is no public record for any of these changes. No sales taxes need be paid because the legal owner is still the same, the original LLC.

TAX CONSEQUENCES OF A TRANSFER

In the previous example, the pickup is never sold. Therefore, there are no transfer fees and *no state sales tax*. I checked this with an attorney. He says a few states may have some obscure regulation about "bulk sales transfers." However, since the state has no way to know about these private transfers—no more than they would know if an envelope of cash was being handed around—his advice was not to worry. However, I cannot guarantee that this is 101 percent legal. To be certain about the regulations in your particular state, check with your legal or accounting expert.

Sale to a third party: Continuing with the example of the pickup, suppose your brother-in-law decides to sell his pickup to a stranger. The buyer will then have two choices. Either he will buy the LLC (and thus save the sales tax) or he will purchase the pickup from the LLC just as he would from anyone else. Most of the time the buyer, unfamiliar with LLCs, will opt to purchase the pickup outright, and that's fine. He is the one that pays the tax, not the seller.

BANK ACCOUNTS AND TAX RETURNS FOR LIMITED-LIABILITY COMPANIES

Income from an LLC flows through to members, which can include domestic or foreign individuals and/or corporations, etc. Therefore, since there is no income, there is no need for the LLC to have a tax identification number (TIN) from the IRS. In fact, the IRS will not know the LLC even exists unless you chose to tell them.

You may, of course, decide to do just that in case you want a bank account in the LLC name. Let us assume that this will be a checking account for a small business and will *not* be interest bearing. In that case:

1. You or your accountant will fill out the simple SS-4 form and send it to the Internal Revenue Service. They will assign you a TIN.

2. You then open the bank account by furnishing a photo-

copy of the LLC's Articles of Organization and giving the new tax identification number.

3. Once this has been done, advise the IRS to cancel the LLC because it will not be used. (And from their viewpoint this is essentially true. The bank will never make a report to the IRS under the TIN because no income is ever generated.)

Until 1997, there was some uncertainty as to how single-member limited-liability companies (LLCs) were to be taxed. However, the IRS has since ruled that a single-member LLC does not need a separate tax ID number because no separate return need be filed. Income (if any) from the LLC is reported on the normal schedule C along with any other "sole proprietor" income. Or, if the single LLC member is a corporation, any income is merely reported as a branch of the operation. Once again, *the LLC does not need a separate tax ID number because no separate return need be filed.*

If you are seriously interested in Level Three privacy, then I suggest you use multiple LLCs in every aspect of your life, including alternate mail addresses, home and car ownership, sideline businesses, whatever!

If you decide to run an actual business in your area with one of your LLCs, then for added liability protection do qualify it to do business in your state. But contract the work among various LLCs, if necessary, to avoid having ten or more employees in a single company and thus subjecting yourself to the federal EP & C Right to Know Act of 1986. [With fifteen employees it gets worse—you'll come under the Civil Rights Act and also the Americans with Disabilities Act.]

QUESTIONS & ANSWERS

What if I open a bank account with my New Mexico LLC but then fail to pay the resident agent?

If you fail to maintain a resident agent, then the LLC will be in default (i.e., no longer "in good standing"). However, the bank will not know this. The only way they could find out would be to call the State Corporation Commission in Santa Fe to inquire, or check the New Mexico Web site. There would seldom be a reason to do so, however.

Many years ago I formed a corporation in a western state, obtained a tax identification number, opened several bank accounts, bought two vehicles, started up a new business, and then transferred the assets to an LLC. I dissolved the corporation and made a final tax return. In the years to follow, I kept and used one of the bank accounts, and to this day I have a leftover GMC pickup that is still in the corporate name. (The same principles apply to an LLC.)

However, I am not saying you should not pay your resident agent. I am merely answering the question above. All things being equal, I suggest you do keep your companies in force by paying the resident agent, just in case someone at a future time *does* check to see if your LLC is in good standing.

Might an LLC be used as a gift?

If you wish to instill the concept of personal privacy into your children, I can think of no better high-school or university graduation gift than a limited-liability company. Think of the privacy that *you* would be enjoying today, had you started working on it right after graduation! Here are two options:

1. If you plan to present the actual documents, the LLC will have to have a name. Why not choose a geographical name from your area? For instance, if you live in San Pedro, California, one of these might work:

- Rolling Hills Associates
- Lomita Limited LC
- Point Fermin Enterprises LC
- Harbor Lake Services LC

2. Present a gift certificate good for one limited-liability company—any name—within the next year. (Any incorporator should be willing to do this.)

13

HIDDEN OWNERSHIP OF VEHICLES AND REAL ESTATE

Things are seldom what they seem/, Skim milk masquerades as cream.

—W.S. GILBERT, *H.M.S. PINAFORE* (1878)

It was less than a year ago that I swung my black Jaguar sedan down the ramp and into a "24-hr. security" parking garage at Seattle's SeaTac Airport, snatched the ticket stub from the attendant, raced for the shuttle bus, and just barely caught my flight to Phoenix. Eight days later I returned to SeaTac, caught the shuttle back to the garage, and joined the check-in line.

When I presented my ticket stub, the cashier hesitated.

"Sir," he said, "Please step to one side. The manager will be right out."

The manager came out, introduced himself, and led me back to his office. I had visions of a scratch in the paint or a ding in a fender.

"The day you left," he said, "your car disappeared."

"Disappeared, as in *stolen?*" (So much for the twenty-four-hour security . . .)

He explained that the same evening I left, one of the attendants parked a car in the stall where my car had been. When he turned the number in to the cashier, the computer showed the stall was already occupied. They quickly searched the entire building to see if my car had been parked in another spot in error. When they failed to find it, they reported it stolen. The next morning the police spotted it, badly damaged, sitting at home plate on a baseball diamond in a Seattle park.

I have the King County Police Vehicle Impound Report before me as I write this. In the Narrative section, line 4, the officer wrote, "*Unable to contact owner.*" Here's why: The car was in the name of an LLC in state A. The address listed for this company was in faraway State B, and a reverse directory failed to show a telephone number at that address.

Although for many years I have been registering my vehicles in the name of limited-liability companies, this was the first time my security precautions had been put to the test. No damage would have been done, of course, had the police been able to contact me in this particular case. However, a short time later my security precautions were to prove worthwhile. As soon as the insurance agent handed me a check for my Jaguar—it was too badly damaged to repair—I bought another car and headed east.

A few days later I arrived in Minneapolis and spent Saturday afternoon visiting used bookstores. It was just getting dark that evening when I pulled out of a parking lot onto West Lake Street, in a hurry because I had to meet a friend from Madrid who was about to arrive at the airport. I failed to see an oncoming motorcycle and almost clipped a Harley being ridden by a three hundred-pound bearded bruiser. He screamed something like "$#*@%&!!," waved his fist, and made violent gestures to have me pull over. (If you've ever been on West Lake Street in south Minneapolis after dark, you know this is not a good neighborhood in which to pull over.)

It was too dark for the rider to see any "so-sorry" gestures—had I made them—so I fed more gas to the horses under the hood. The overweight biker followed me right on to 35W going south, with all the time in the world to memorize my license number. Although I do not scare easily, this time I was seriously alarmed, enough to set a new Minnesota speed record between West Thirty-fifth and the I-494 junction, where I cut the lights and peeled off at the exit. Whether he memorized the number or not, and whether he was carrying a gun or not, once I lost the biker I was safe forever—the plates would lead him nowhere. But my heart was still thumping when I pulled into airport parking.

Five Saturdays later I was in Londonderry, New Hampshire, to meet Carl Prague, an old friend who used to live aboard the *Raider*, a 1912, wooden sailboat with Santa Cruz de Tenerife (Canary Islands) as a home base. A stiff wind was blowing when we stopped at the Country Market on Highway 102 to pick up some wine and snacks, and when we came out, a few abandoned shopping carts were starting to move. Just as we were putting the groceries in the car a hard gust sent a cart racing past us and across the parking lot directly toward a parked Honda Civic with a man and a woman in it. There was no way to stop it, and we watched as it struck the driver's door with a resounding clang and bounced back. As we continued to watch, we could see that the woman was obviously screaming at the man to do something, and the "something" turned out to be a trip over to see me. Assuming he wanted some help, I lowered my window halfway as he came around my side, and said hello.

"Your cart hit my car!"

"Excuse me? We didn't have a cart."

"Yes you did, and we saw it come from here."

At least he didn't weigh more than 140, and my friend Carl is an ex-wrestler, so this time I was just amused, not scared.

"*I wrote down your license number,*" the man muttered, brandishing a scrap of paper, "and you'll hear from my lawyer."

Well, best of luck, buddy, and have a nice day.

PURCHASING A VEHICLE WITH AN LLC

It is easier than you think. (If you skipped Chapter 12, now would be a good time to go back and read it.) My clients, nevertheless, are often reluctant to start using limited-liability companies because they have never done it before.

One such person was Jim in San Francisco, who asked me to help him purchase a used Lincoln Town Car with almost no miles on it. It was for sale by a private party in Washington and Jim wanted to title it in that state for personal reasons. He asked for my help because he was not sure he could handle the registration and yet keep his name out of it. Here is the transaction step-by-step.

1. Since Jim was in a hurry, I pulled a New Mexico "shelf" LLC from my files that I'll call Golden Gateway LC. (A shelf LLC is one that has been formed in the past for future use, and just put "on the shelf" until needed. I recommend this procedure to all readers, and personally keep shelf LLCs on hand at all times.) We then flew to Seattle, rented a car, and drove out to Port Angeles to make the deal.

2. The seller, a ninety-seven-year-old (!) woman who had purchased the car in 1991 and then stored it, signed off on the title. She also signed the bill of sale I had prepared beforehand. We filled in Golden Gateway LC as the buyer and gave a ghost address that Jim had already set up through a friend in Cheyenne, Wyoming.

3. Rather than go to the Department of Motor Vehicles in
Port Angeles, we checked the yellow pages under "Licensing Services" and picked a private licensing bureau. (They
charge a small fee for handling the paperwork but are easier to deal with than state employees.) Jim went through
the line with me, but only as an observer. He wanted to
see how I would answer the questions.

> *Clerk:* "What's the UBI number for this company?"
> [Washington requires an ID number for all legal
> entities doing business in their state.]
>
> *Me:*   "Golden Gateway LC doesn't do business in this
> state, and Wyoming doesn't require a UBI num-
> ber."
>
> *Clark:* "Then why not license it in Wyoming?"
> *Me:*   "For at least six months the car will be in this
> state, and the law requires we therefore license
> it here." [100 percent correct, always.]

The clerk accepted that, and then asked me for ID. I explained
that the car was *not for me* but for the company, and showed her
the LLC's Articles of Organization. She let that pass, but had a
number of some sort been needed, she could have typed in the six-
digit filing number written at the top of the Articles. She then
pushed a computer printout over to me and showed me where to
sign. I scrawled an illegible signature that matched the one on the
bill of sale (although she didn't ask to see it).

> *Clerk:* "Print your title after your signature, please."

Since I was neither a member nor a manager of Jim's newly
acquired company, I printed in "Sales Mgr." (Jim retroactively
appointed me "Sales Manager for a Day.") We paid the various

license and transfer fees in cash and were on our way. What had been accomplished?

First and foremost, total privacy. Suppose a private investigator sees Jim's car parked in Las Vegas at what he considers a suspicious address. He makes a note of the Washington license plate, and obtains whatever information is on file with the Department of Motor Vehicles in Olympia. He will get the name "Golden Gateway LC" and an address in Wyoming, nothing more. If the PI then calls the Secretary of State's office in Cheyenne, he will learn that it is not a Wyoming company. That leaves him forty-nine states plus the District of Columbia to check out. Even if he eventually calls Santa Fe, the records in New Mexico will reveal only the name of the resident agent. If he contacted the resident agent, he would learn that the agent does not give out information without a subpoena. If he were able to serve a fake subpoena (unlikely), he would get an address in the Canary Islands from the agent because that is the address I use for all shelf companies. And trust me on this one—the Canary Islands address is the end of the line.

Second: If Jim so wishes, ownership can be transferred to one of his companies, or to a friend, with *no sales tax* (explained in Chapter 12).

SUMMARY: TITLES IN THE NAME OF AN LLC

LLCs are ideal for titling the following:

- Cars, trucks, tractors, motorcycles.
- Snowmobiles, boats, utility trailers.
- RVs, travel trailers, pickup campers.

How many LLCs are needed? Although I use a separate limited-liability company for every purchase, many will consider this as overkill. The other extreme would be to use a single LLC for all purchases. There is no serious problem with this. The two minor drawbacks are:

1. You cannot transfer ownership of a single item by transferring ownership of the LLC because everything is titled together.

2. If a PI is searching for assets and discovers that you own—for example—a boat in the name of an LLC, he will then search state records for any other titles in the same name . . . and discover the other things you own.

Many of my clients work with four companies: They use the first for their principal car, van, or SUV, the second for an additional vehicle, the third for real estate other than their home, and the fourth for everything else.

HIDING OWNERSHIP OF YOUR RESIDENCE

The best way to purchase a home is with a revocable trust, especially where a mortgage is involved. (See Chapter 10.) A trust is not a do-it-yourself project—use a tax attorney or a CPA who has experience with estate planning.

When you decide to purchase a new home, much more is involved, of course, than merely the name on the title deed. The true example that follows [names have been changed] brings everything together:

AN ACTUAL MOVE, STEP-BY-STEP

The following account is of an actual move by two of my readers who shall here be referred to as Harold and Helen Bond. They decided to move to a small city two counties removed, since many records are kept by county only, with no cross-references to other counties. The purpose of this move was to make a complete break with all past records. I'll call their previous home Old-City in Old-County, and the move will be to New-City in New-County.

Before they started, here are some questions they asked themselves, and the answers they came up with. (It is vital to make these decisions beforehand.)

- When asked for our present address, what will that be? [*A ghost address at the far end of the state.*]
- When asked for our present telephone number, what shall we say? [*We just had the telephone disconnected as we are selling our home.*]
- When getting a new cell phone number, what will be the reason? [*We are often in this area to see friends and would like a local number.*]
- When getting a new local ghost address for mail, what excuse will we give? [*We plan to move to this area but will often be traveling and we need a permanent address.*]

The Bonds have a history of making fast decisions. Within a week they located a nearly new home in New-County, with no close neighbors. It was listed for $219,500 and had been on the market for six months. The Bonds contacted the listed agent. Before writing up the offer, they explained to the agent that they valued their privacy. Therefore, neither of their names was to appear on any written document whatsoever. The offer was then made in the name of a trust they had already had drawn up: the Cheyenne Valley Trust. As trustee, Helen Bond signed her maiden name, "Helen Hennesy."

The owner, an elderly woman no longer able to live alone, was given just three hours to accept or refuse an offer of $200,000, with $50,000 payable at the close. Jim, the real-estate agent, explained to her that the buyers would pay the balance due in one year or less, and until that time they would make monthly payments of approximately $1,000, representing interest only on the loan, at the rate of 10 percent. [No Social Security number could be given and thus no credit check. But none was needed. If the Bonds defaulted, she would keep the $50,000 down.] She accepted the offer. The Bonds now had a year in which to sell their old home and pay off the private note. (When the seller owns his or her own home, it is very common to carry part of the loan for a short period of time. It is also perfectly safe because the seller takes a first mortgage or deed of trust against the property for the amount of the loan.)

When the title company learned that title would be taken in the name of a trust, and signed by one trustee only, they asked for a copy of the trust. Although the trust document showed the trustees to be Harold and Helen Bond, it contained this clause: "Helen Bond may sign any legal document with her maiden name, Helen Hennesy, and this will have the same legal validity as if she had signed her name as Helen Bond." (This means the name Bond does not appear in the court system. It remains hidden in the copy of the trust, which resides only in the files of the title company.)

Insurance: All previous insurance had been carried via State Farm. The new home was insured in New-City but the insurance on the vehicles was left with the State Farm agent in Old-City. State Farm allows this, providing both agents are in the same state. (An agent from one area cannot tap into the computer from another area.) Thus, the State Farm agent in Old-City did not learn the address of the new residence.

New telephone number: Harold Bond called GTE for "new residential service," said his name was Martin Johnson, and asked for two lines with unpublished numbers. He gave the true address for installation and his ghost address for the billing address.

"And your Social Security number, Mr. Johnson?"

"I never use my Social Security number for identification."

"In that case you will have to go to our GTE phone store in New-City Mall and identify yourself with picture ID. They'll give you a receipt with a code number, and as soon as you have it, call us back."

Harold put on a suit and tie and showed up at the phone

store. Both a male and a female were at the counter. He recalled reading that PIs after information always say a male PI should pick a female clerk, and vice versa. He explained his "problem" to the female clerk.

"My name is Harold Bond but for many years I've been writing articles about home security for national magazines and my telephone is always listed in my pen name, Martin Johnson."

"Well, we need to know who you really are."

"Of course, and here's my passport."

Once his identity was established with the passport, he was given a code number and assured that the telephone would be listed in their computers as Martin Johnson.

With the receipt in hand, Bond called GTE again. He identified himself as Martin Johnson, said he had been to their phone store, and now had a code number. He gave this number, and was told that all was now well, and that the two new numbers would be in service within five business days. (It is not always that easy. If you have a telephone company like U.S. West, you may need a nominee.)

Propane gas: A propane tank was already in use at the new home so Helen Bond called the company to transfer the billing name to Cheyenne Valley Trust. When asked for her name, she gave it as Helen Hennesy. All bills were to go to the ghost address.

Power company: A phone call for a change from the previous owner to Cheyenne Valley Trust was all it took. No deposit required.

Garbage pickup: In some areas this can be extremely difficult, but when Helen called the company in New-City she was merely asked for the new name and billing address. (I once tried to arrange for garbage pickup in a rural area, but the clerk was adamant. She refused to consider a cash deposit. "Social Security number or no pickup!" I ended up hauling our garbage to the local sanitary landfill on a regular basis, rather than look for a nominee.)

Library card: Every move presents different problems. In this case, the Bonds found that getting a library card was as difficult as the garbage pickup was easy. There are five libraries in New-County—each with financial difficulties—and the rural areas are divided among the city libraries. Cards from one library cannot be used at any other library. Non–city residents must not only pay a forty-dollar annual fee but must show picture ID *along with proof that they reside at an address within the library's territory*. The Bonds left this one till last. Then Harold showed up with suit, tie, title insurance for his new home (Cheyenne Valley Trust), and his passport. Since the phone book showed a number of Bond families in the county, Harold filled out the application as "Stanley Bond," since the passport showed Stanley as his middle name.

"Your telephone number, Stanley?"

"Sorry, but we don't have one yet."

"Well, we need the last four digits for a pin number."

"You can use 1812, from the last phone we had." (Actually just an easy-to-remember number: the War of 1812.)

Technically, this violated the rule of never, ever having your name and your true address listed together. However, the Bonds did not worry about it because:

- They had already checked, and learned that the five county libraries do not exchange information with one another.

- They knew from the local telephone book that there were seventeen Bonds *listed*, and a good guess would be at least ten more Bond families unlisted. Anyone looking for "Harold" would not recognize "Stanley" because Harold had never used his middle name in Old-City.

- The library did not have Harold's Social Security number, nor his date of birth.

At the present time, no one is after the Bonds (as far as they know). However, suppose for whatever reason, someone named Heinrich from a previous life decides to track them down and sue them. He goes to a PI for help and the PI starts running the names Harold Bond and Helen Bond through computer databases. Nothing will show up in court records, nor in utilities, nor telephone records. Nothing in national databases for magazine subscriptions (other than persons with the same name, of course). Nothing under vehicle ownership. Nothing from the DMV in the present state, since the Bonds use out-of-state licenses. At this point, rather than start spending tens of thousands of dollars to continue, Heinrich will most likely call off the search.

QUESTIONS & ANSWERS

I just moved from Denver to Miami. Since I am keeping my Colorado driver's license should I also keep my Colorado license plates?

This question comes up constantly, and the answer is, "it depends." Leslie L—— is one of my clients. Les works for a well-known electronics company in California's Silicon Valley. He also happens to live there but he licensed his new Porsche in Texas (big tax savings) and obtained a Texas driver's license. He does have a ghost address in Texas and he knows the area around Plano.

One day he was stopped and questioned by the California Highway Patrol. The officer did not accept his story of being from Texas. He was ordered to obtain California plates within thirty days or face a serious penalty. Rather than accept this, Les went to court.

"I'm a Texas resident," he said. "The officer made a mistake. Here is my Texas driver's license with my Texas home address." The judge accepted this explanation and Les kept his Texas plates. Two months later, Les was in a commuter parking lot taking a nap in his car.

"A cop woke me up and was suspicious of the Texas plates and my Texas driver's license. He asked me a lot of questions about what I was doing and how long had I been out here. I simply said, 'I'm a Texas resident working out here temporarily.' He called it in, and everything was okay, so he left me alone."

However, I suspect that with a few more experiences like this, Les will bite the bullet and pay the costly fee for California plates.

Can I have both local and out-of state license plates for the same car?

Absolutely—in fact, I currently have dual plates for one of my own cars. It was originally purchased and registered in State A. I also licensed it in State B, where I own a home. I explained to the clerk at the licensing bureau that I was keeping my old registration as well, because I spend half of my time back there.

"But then," said the clerk, "you will have to pay the annual registration fees in *both* states." I assured her that was no problem. Here is why I keep two plates:

Local plate: This way I have no problems with nosy neighbors or the local cops.

Out-of-state plate: I get out the screwdriver and switch plates only for short periods of time. One of these times is when I arrange to meet persons who have no idea I live in the area. They assume I am just passing through on a trip. In fact, I call attention to the plate when I make the appointment: "I'll meet you at Denny's at Exit 34. Watch for a black sedan with [State B] plates."

This is also the plate I would put on if I were going to meet with someone I did not trust. For example, a bent PI with an equally bent pal in the police department who might someday be asked to put out a watch for my car. (They would search in vain for a car with the State B plates, because the plates for that car would be hidden back in my garage.)

Summary: I highly recommend the use of dual plates for Level Three privacy.

I own several very expensive collector cars and it would cost a fortune to pay the sales tax if I retitled them in the

names of limited-liability companies. The registrations are in my name and with my true address. Any suggestions?

In the long term, you may wish to sell your cars. When you buy more, title them with LLCs not only for privacy but for tax-free transfers as explained in Chapter 12. Meanwhile, when you next pay your annual fee, turn in a change of address. The ghost address should not be traceable back to you, and must show on the registration certificate. That way, anyone looking for you will be led astray.

Warning: Learn from a mistake made by Ira G——, one of my newer clients who is a divorced attorney in a Chicago suburb. His first move was to change the address on the registration for each of his collector cars. One of them was a Triumph stored at a friend's house about an hour's drive from where he lives. He handled the change of address by mail and did not get around to driving over to take the old registration out of the glove compartment. About the same time the ghost address was registered, his Triumph disappeared. Ira did not discover this fact for about two months and when he did, the thief appeared to be someone in a dispute with the friend. Ira called the thief, who turned out to be an ex–Hell's Angel on a first-name basis with local authorities. An argument ensued in which the thief claimed he took the car from the friend's garage in payment of a debt. He was furious with the lawyer for threatening him. Can you see it coming? This ex–Hell's Angel guy had the car with the old registration in it, which showed *the home address* of the lawyer's wife, where she lived alone with their young son.

Would this be a good time for you to go through the glove compartments of your vehicles, collector-type or otherwise?

What do you think about vanity license plates?

Personally, I prefer not to use vanity plates because they draw attention to the driver. If you do decide on a vanity plate, you may wish to copy one of two plates I've seen and liked. The first was seen on a new Jaguar several years ago: 000-000. Last month

I saw the second—strangely enough, it was on *another* new Jaguar: NO NMBR.

Will hiding my true address and having license plates that cannot be traced protect me from stalkers?

You mean, like, "guaranteed"? When it comes to privacy and security, there are few if any guarantees, but the precautions you mention will certainly balance the odds in your favor. According to a 1997 National Institute of Justice study, one in twelve American women is stalked at least once, and stalkers pursue or harass at least 1 million women every year. The telephone survey, which contacted 8,000 women and 8,000 men, found that 8.1 percent of women surveyed and 2.2 percent of the men reported that they had been stalked at least once. According to the study, only half the victims in the study said they reported the episode to the police. Of women who obtained restraining orders against stalkers, 80 percent reported that these orders were violated.

Note that men as well as women may be stalked, and four times out of five, going to the police does not help. Even though you follow every instruction in this book one danger still remains—the danger of being spotted *and then followed*. If the stalker knows where you play, work, or worship, or who and where your friends are, he (or a PI in his employ) can follow you home.

Is there a remedy? Not entirely, unless you are never located in the first place. If you have to meet with the stalker, such as in court, you may be followed, and there is always the danger that the stalker or his agent will be successful. On the other hand, ask any private investigator the greatest problem he faces when doing surveillance and you'll learn that the danger is that the victim is *aware*. Perhaps not aware of any specific thing, but just aware in general. Looking around when walking, watching the mirrors when driving, etc.

Carjackers say the same thing—many crimes would have been avoided had the victims been aware of their approach. In my own case, I never allow any specific car to follow me for a period of time in rural areas (where my homes invariably are). I drive a few miles over the speed limit and if a car comes up behind me I turn on the right turn signal, slow down, and force him to pass. There are a few other measures I take, as well, but you get the idea.

If you live in a city and think a certain car is following you, make four right turns, i.e., go around the block. If the car you've seen in your mirrors follows you, *do not go home*. Drive to the nearest police station or fire station or to a well-lighted gas station with a number of cars filling up. Hopefully you have your cell phone with you, in which case you can dial 911.

If a stalker can be identified, why not recommend that someone just beat him up?

The author of a series of books on street fighting reviewed this chapter and recommends just that. To quote from his last e-mail:

> Stalked women should immediately get a man (husband, boyfriend, father, uncle, godfather, etc.) to take out the stalker. I've done it twice. With the first guy, I followed him into the men's room of a bar (where I knew the bouncer and didn't have to worry about the complications), and, quite literally, beat the s——out of him. I left him with the warning, "Walk into the same room with her, and I'll feed you to my dogs." With the other guy, I cornered him in an elevator and gave him a choice: either break his lease and move out of the building in which the woman lived, or I was taking him to the roof for a little 20-story diving practice.

However, I do not recommend this procedure to others because:

1. It is illegal (which is why I haven't named the well-known author). You could be sued or go to jail.

2. If the stalker survives the beating, he may kill his target in revenge, then kill himself.

What precautions can be taken against carjackers?

Privacy and security go together. In the words of the Los Angeles Police Department—referring to carjackings—"Don't give up your privacy." In other words, *never* get into your own car at gunpoint. Just pretend to faint (or maybe do it for real!) and fall down, limp.

Here's a scam I recently heard about (again). It's an oldie, but still works. A new Mercedes was parked at a Minnesota shopping mall one foggy morning and someone reported to the office that the lights on a white Mercedes, license plate so-and-so, had been left on. When the owner showed up the lights were *not* on—and she was robbed at gunpoint and the car taken.

Female drivers, when alone, attract more attention than males. One solution is to tint your windows as dark—or darker—than the law allows. Then have a male mannequin in the passenger seat. In fact, with dark enough tinting you may even get by with one of those rubber masks from a costume store. Just slip it over the headrest—can't hurt, might help. (Just don't use this gag for the car-pool lane, however. There are a few cops out there without an adequate sense of humor.)

While on this subject, I have an article from the *Skagit Valley Herald*, dated January 10, 1998, and titled "Accused Rapist had been Jailed."

> According to police, the man rammed his car into the woman's vehicle about 7 P.M. Wednesday. The woman later told police she got out and the man then pushed her into his own car, climbed in, and drove south . . . he beat her up and raped her.

Hint to you husbands: note the words "*she got out.*" Might this be a good time to review security with your wife, and make sure she always keeps her doors locked and has her cell phone with her?

14

BANK ACCOUNTS AND MONEY TRANSFERS

If you can't convince them, confuse them.

—HARRY S. TRUMAN

Any bank account you have in your own name (in whatever state), tied in with your Social Security number, can be tracked down by agencies specializing in asset searches for lawyers. This includes certificates of deposit as well as IRA accounts.

Robert O'Harrow, Jr., from the *Washington Post*, writes that "lawyers, debt collectors, and private investigators buy the data to help in civil lawsuits, divorces, and other financial matters. Prices range from just over $100 to several thousand dollars for a look at banks nationwide and a report that includes information about stocks, mutual funds, and safe-deposit boxes." O'Harrow relates the account of a security official at BankBoston ". . . who noticed an ad for one of the services and anonymously ordered a search on himself. When the report came back, the official, Frederick Tilley, said he learned new details about his own accounts. 'They came back with the account information, down to the penny,' said Tilley. 'There are lots of them and it's freely advertised.' "

For pages and pages of advertisements with headings like AS-SETS LOCATED and WE'LL SHOW YOU THE MONEY! see *P.I. Magazine* (listed in Appendix I) or *California Lawyer*. Copies of the individual checks themselves may also be obtained, since all checks are microfilmed front and back. This reveals not only payees and endorsers but also memos (if any) and signatures.

If you are the subject of the search, what will the computers reveal? Do you wish to be identified as one with deep pockets, or would you prefer to be considered judgment-proof (i.e., with not enough assets worth suing you for)?

Or suppose, with no forewarning, you find yourself under investigation by someone who wishes to cause you harm. This could be anyone from an ex-employee to a disgruntled present or former mate. A private detective may come up with infor-mation from so far in the past that you had forgotten it was there. Imagine that you are forced via *subpoena duces tecum* to turn over all bank records for the past three years. Are there *any* checks, *any* charges, that you would prefer to remain secret? (Think about this carefully. Consider newsletter sub-scriptions, contributions, trips, purchases of alcohol, guns, am-munition, or whatever. Consider rentals, from autos to motels to videos.)

Yes, I know that small ads run continually in small offbeat newsletters and magazines, or in direct mail offers, with a head-ing like:

OPEN A BANK ACCOUNT WITHOUT
A SOCIAL SECURITY NUMBER

The cost is usually $10. I answer these ads just to be sure that something new hasn't been discovered. To date, nothing has. The reports tell you to attempt to open a bank account but to state that you will not give your Social Security number. The bank representative then refuses to proceed, at which point you threaten to sue the bank, listing rather generic legal references designed to intimidate. To satisfy your curiosity and to save you ten dollars—the bank will refuse to open such an account.

Nevertheless, all is not lost. Difficult? Yes. Hopeless? No. I have been involved in the secret use of bank accounts in the U.S. and/or offshore since 1959 and have not experienced any serious problems.

As I said in the previous section, since we are discussing privacy measures rather than tax evasion, you need have no secrets from the IRS. This report is about hiding bank accounts from your enemies, *not* from the IRS. Some of my suggestions that follow may be offbeat and perhaps underhanded. I agree, but they are not currently, nor are they anticipated to become *illegal*, according to my American attorney, who reviews all my projects.

USE A NOMINEE

This method requires the assistance of a relative or friend. Let's call this person Sally Faith. Sally can open a bank account in her own name or as the principal in a trust, a corporation, or a limited-liability company. (We assume Sally is such a low-profile person that no one would ever bother to sue her.) Let's assume you wish to have her open this account in her own name. Here are the steps:

1. Choose an independent bank in a state where neither you nor Sally lives. This will isolate both of you from routine searches and will hide Sally's possible death (should such occur) from the bank authorities long enough for you to cash a final check, closing out all but the last $10 from the account.

2. Prepare Sally for obvious questions such as, "Since you live in California, why are you opening this account here in Pioche, Nevada?" The answer might be "I'm thinking about moving here within the next three months."

3. Withdraw cash from your present account(s), perhaps $1,000. Purchase a bank cashier's check from a bank where you are *not* known, made out to Sally Faith and with a fictitious remitter.

4. Next, Sally practices, hour after hour, an indecipherable signature, the kind businessmen use all over Europe. She then assembles the necessary identification (a passport is best, if she has one, since it gives far less information than a driver's license), travels to the city where the bank is located, and opens the account. She accepts a few temporary checks and deposit slips but does *not* order checks through the bank. *You* order them from a mail-order company such as Checks in the Mail (1-800-773-4443) or Current Checks (1-800-533-3973). Use a starting number of 8001 or higher, so that the account appears to have been established years ago. Order any printed name you like, such as "S. F. Services," and either list no address at all or just any city and state you prefer. When the checks come—hopefully enough to last you for years—Sally sits down and signs them until her signatures start to vary. Time out for coffee or Dr Pepper, then she continues to sign, with breaks, until finished.

5. You, of course, keep all the checks, either well hidden or under lock and key. From this point on you use these pre-signed checks in any way you please. (For deposits, order and use a rubber stamp.)

I suggest you keep the balance reasonably low. Open a non-interest-bearing account so that there will be no report to the IRS. Perhaps you pay Sally a flat fee for setting things up, and then pay her $100 an hour if you need her services later on, such as for signing new checks. Allowing five seconds per signature, plus short breaks to rest her fingers, she should be able to sign five hundred checks within an hour.

A CORPORATE BANK ACCOUNT

Ads are constantly running in *Inc.* magazine, the *Wall Street Journal* and other publications by incorporators such as Laughlin Associates (Nevada) and CorpCo (Delaware). They offer to form a corporation for you that in many cases will include a corporate bank account.

Beware! If you are actually going to *do business* in your own area, which does not happen to be either Delaware or Nevada, then the out-of-state corporation will have to be "qualified to do business" in your own state. It will be simpler and cheaper to form your own corporation (or limited-liability company) in your home state, and that is, in fact, what I suggest you do.

However, if you are *not* going to be doing business locally, then the ideal state for incorporating is not Delaware or Nevada, but Wyoming. Both Nevada and Delaware draw too much attention, both require corporate identifiers such as Inc. or Ltd., and the IRS audits more corporations in Nevada (owing to prior abuses) than in any other state. Nevertheless, whichever state is used, you will be subject to complex tax rules and regulations, and under a general obligation to hold corporate meetings and keep corporate minutes. If opening a normal bank account is your *sole* objective, then an LLC will serve your purposes better than a corporation. But sometimes other factors do enter in, so let's consider this subject a bit more:

In Wyoming you can form a corporation with *no corporate identifier!* Yes, you can form corporations and open bank accounts there in names such as WOLFGANG AMADEUS, OLIVER JOHN SIMPSON, or J. SMITH.

However, I know of no Wyoming bank that will open an account for anyone who *admits* to being from out of state. If, therefore, you travel to that state to open a bank account, first arrange to have a local address.

You will find additional information about corporations and limited-liability companies in Chapters 11 and 12.

OR, OPEN NO BANK ACCOUNT AT ALL

Hundreds of thousands of American citizens, as well as a similar number of illegal aliens, manage to live without any bank account at all, and not all are financially disadvantaged. This is one way to ensure that you do not reveal the name of your bank when you write a check for the rent, the mortgage, utilities, taxes, or home repair.

Worse, there is a real danger if you ever write a check to a lawyer, CPA, or anyone else who—unknown to you—is a crook. When investigating this person—perhaps surreptitiously—government agents will come up with a copy of your check. Might this possibly lead to *your* mail and bank account being examined? Or a tap on *your* telephone?

Therefore, you may decide to pay professionals in cash if you're there in person. If not, you might mail a postal money order, a cashier's check, or a traveler's check. For small payments, I recommend the money orders sold in convenience stores or at Western Union offices. They are economical, can be purchased with no ID, and the line for the payee is left blank. You fill in the payee on your own. The issuing office has no record of the sender or the receiver. There may be a limit of $500 or $700 for each money order but you can purchase several at a time.

For amounts larger than $2,000, you may prefer a bank money order or cashier's check. Many banks do not require ID when you are purchasing the checks with cash. If in doubt, check out a bank beforehand, asking them about their policies. Or test their policy by purchasing a small check to pay for something you are going to order by mail. If asked for ID, tell the absolute truth: "I didn't bring any ID with me; I didn't think I'd need it."

HAWALA BANKING

This is the oldest banking system in existence, used for exchanging money across international borders. Since no money actually *moves* anywhere, it cannot be traced. Yes, you read correctly, *it cannot be traced.*

Although it is widely practiced among Chinese and Indians (from India), and to a lesser extent by Spaniards, the average American has never heard of it. The easiest way to explain it is to review a transaction I had in the late 1960s when I flew to Madrid and then to Boston on business. While in the latter city, I was invited to a cocktail party and when it came up that I lived in Spain I was introduced to a short, grossly fat attorney I'll here refer to as Cabot. After initial pleasantries, I was guided over to a secluded area where the following conversation took place.

"Jack," he said, "maybe one hand can wash another here. I had a client from Barcelona who ran out of convertible pesetas. [Only convertible pesetas—governed by strict rules—can be sent out of the country.] So this guy paid me by giving me title to an apartment he had near the beach in Alicante. I had a friend sell it for me, but it was in normal pesetas, understand?"

"Yes, you can't take the money out. How much, in pesetas?"

"Two million nine," said Cabot, which at that time was equivalent to about $47,000. "Can we do a little trade here, maybe?"

"Well," I answered, stalling, "sometimes I have the same problem myself. Why not just spend the money over there?"

"Listen, not to offend you or anything, but I've been to Spain twice, and all in one trip. The *first* time and the *last* time. I made some joke about Franco and those guys with the triangle hats almost took away my passport! So look, Jack, can we work something out? Like at ten percent?"

"Thirty-two thousand is about all I've got, in dollars."

"C'mon, you got another five somewhere. Thirty-seven K and it's a done deal!"

Because both Cabot and I trusted a mutual acquaintance there, we did the deal in his office the following morning. I gave

Cabot a check for $37,000 drawn on a Londonderry, New Hampshire, bank (presigned by a nominee), and received in return his check, drawn on his account in Spain and made out to *Portador* for 2,900,000 pesetas. (*Portador* means "bearer." In those happy days almost *all* checks in Spain were made out to the bearer!) It cost me an extra day and some travel money to return to the Canaries via Barcelona, but Cabot's check was good. I took the money in cash from Banco Hispano Americano, lugging it back to the airport in a zipper case. This is the procedure known from ancient times as hawala, sometimes spelled hawalah, and occasionally referred to as hundi. Let's review the procedure:

- There are no written documents, the exchanges are based on mutual trust (perhaps for that reason unpopular in the U.S.?).

- Only local currencies are used. If you are sending money to the UK, for example, you'll pay the U.S. hawala banker in dollars and receive pounds in London.

- This exchange cannot be traced—no money crosses a border. The hawala system is never advertised, and may sort of, like, skirt some laws or regulations. However, it does make for interesting conversations among friends. Beyond that, proceed at your own risk.

QUESTIONS & ANSWERS

What if a bank requires my thumbprint on the back of a check?

I've never given a thumbprint at a bank. If they ask for it, I go to another bank or endorse it over to a third party (perhaps the nominee for an account I set up) and deposit it to that account. However, here are a couple of points to keep in mind:

- As long as the check does not bounce, and assuming it is not written on a small bank where the check is returned to the client, the check disappears into the bank archives forever.

- If you do give your thumb print, press hard and slightly twist your thumb. Practice at home first. The goal is to smear the print just a trace. If done right, this will make a match impossible, and yet the clerk may not notice it at all.

There is also such a thing as filling in the grooves of your thumbprint with glue, then allowing it to dry. Then a second coating is given and while still moist you press it against the thumb of another person. But I don't think you need to get into all that, unless you are on the FBI's top ten list.

Although I do wish to keep my private life private, I am not paranoid. Can't I just keep a normal bank account and a credit card—both in my own name—and get by?

My answer may surprise you. Yes you may. I do urge you, however, to follow these suggestions:

1. Open a new account in another state, any place where you can give a local address. (That of a friend? A relative?) Use your passport rather than your driver's license, because the driver's license will tip them off that you are not local, and many banks will not open an account if you live out of the area. Try to avoid it, but it may be that the new bank will ask to check with your previous bank. Use your own judgment on this.

2. Once the new account is open, close your present account(s) to block the back trail.

3. Choose the smallest possible bank, preferably with no out-of-state branches. This may reduce the number of databases your name will be in.

4. Later, if necessary, you can change the address for the monthly statements to your ghost address, but let a few months go by first. In a cover letter, give some reason for the change. Perhaps you will be "back and forth" and the ghost address is more convenient. Or perhaps the address is for your accountant, who handles your financial matters.

5. Never, ever, as long as you live, reveal your true address and telephone number to anyone at the new bank.

6. Do not use the checks the bank gives you. Order your own by mail. Either leave the upper-left corner blank, or give one of your initials plus a last name. Do not list any address or phone number.

15

HOW TO SECRETLY RUN A HOME-BASED BUSINESS

A little inaccuracy sometimes saves tons of explanation.
—SAKI, *THE SQUARE EGG* (1924)

"ARE YOU ZONED FOR BUSINESS?" That was the title of an article in *Home Office Computing* about two years ago. The subtitle was "Registering your home office is a difficult but necessary evil."

In Chapter 1, you will recall that I said, ". . . if I mention any procedure which I suspect might be construed as illegal in some states or provinces, I will warn you of that fact beforehand and let you make your own decision." When it comes to working at home without registering for a business license, consider yourself warned.

The authorities seldom if ever send out patrols to search for violators. Rather, they depend upon tips from your competitors or complaints from the neighbors. Further, the usual result of a complaint is merely a warning, so stay cool and keep these tips in mind:

- Never, ever tell your neighbors about your business.
- Do not have your customers or clients come to your home.
- Never receive deliveries at home—but then, you already knew that. The best invisible business is run by mail, fax, phone, e-mail, and/or the Internet. Receipts can be cash and money orders, deposited in various nominee accounts. There will be no bounced checks. No one will know your age, race, background, or if you're a first cousin to the Roswell aliens.

You can sell such a business to someone else in any state or—in some cases—any nation in the world. In 1989, one of my clients started a mail-order business from the spare bedroom in his cheap tract house in a small town in Nevada. The initial investment was $1,500. The product had to do with a paralegal service that was attractive to Europeans. The first year all he did was break even, so he lived on his savings. Then sales began to grow by word of mouth. In 1992 he withdrew a six-figure bonus (using a convoluted tax-free transaction) and kept working. In 1994, a privacy-oriented entrepreneur from Nebraska purchased 100 percent of *the stock in the corporation that owned the customer list for* $500,000. I was there along with the lawyers at the time of the sale.

Not a single neighbor knew a business had been run from that home, much less that he had been netting up to $20,000 a month before taxes. And the taxes weren't all that much—90 percent of the stock was in a charitable remainder trust, not subject to income tax. (See Chapter 11.) However, the basic reason for starting the business was *privacy*. The fact that it did better than expected was a bonus.

SHOULD YOU WORK "OFF THE BOOKS"?

Millions do it, and it certainly gives you privacy . . . unless, of course, you are caught. Nothing very private about getting arrested! I have never evaded income taxes nor have I ever recommended that course to anyone else. Why cheat and run the risk of a jail sentence when there are so many ways to make money and keep enough for yourself legally?)

Loompanics Unlimited (Port Townsend, Washington) publishes a small paperback book titled *How to Do Business "Off the Books,"* by "Adam Cash." There are enough warnings about the IRS in this book to make you more fearful *after* reading it than you were before!

Paladin Press (Boulder, Colorado) publishes a similar book, *Ragnar's Guide to the Underground Economy.* The author lists such occupations as housecleaning, dog grooming, boat repair, hauling, tree removal, critter control, locksmithing, yard work, window washing, pet care, house-sitting, photography, carpentry, gunsmithing, chimney sweeping, roofing, and bookkeeping. An examination of the individual stories told indicates an average annual income of less than $30,000.

Don't even *think* about working "off the books."

ANONYMOUS PROFITS IN REAL ESTATE

Years ago I ran across an aging landlord from Chesapeake, Virginia, named Lonnie Scruggs. For the past ten years he had been buying old—and I do mean *old*—mobile homes for a few thousand dollars each. He then doubled or tripled the price and financed them at up to 18 percent annual interest. The reason this worked was because his low-income buyers had only two questions: (1) How much down? (2) How much a month? These deals were easy to sell because down payments were about $500, and monthly payments were less than $200. (Buyers paid rent to the mobile home park on their own.) Here's why it's so great from the standpoint of privacy:

- You purchase the mobile home for CASH so no one asks you for credit information.
- You title it in the name of a limited-liability company.
- The buyer—if he doesn't make his payments in cash (many do!)—will make out the check to whatever name you say.

I assumed Scruggs had retired by now, but I recently ran across a copy of A. D. Kessler's *Creative Real Estate* magazine and I see he writes a column now for Kessler, and gives seminars teaching his system. I note, also, that his two books are still in print.

INVISIBLE PROFILE

In general, the idea behind running any low-profile business is to keep your name out of the picture, so that you cannot be named in a lawsuit. You will, therefore, run the business in another name. It can be in the name of a nominee only, or with a business license citing the nominee as the principal. However, a better way is to use a limited-liability company. In fact, some persons use *two* LLCs, with the first one doing business and the second one as the sole member of the first. A totally different method is to use one or more established businesses as a "front," and I just recently dealt with such a business in Boston. Here's some background information.

Thirty years ago I went to the Bombay Bazaar in Las Palmas, Gran Canaria, to buy a new watch. At that time, Bulova was at the cutting edge of time-keeping technology with their electronic Accutron model. Instead of tick-tick-tick from a balance move-ment, the Accutrons emitted a pleasing low-level hum from a tuning fork, and the sweep second hand moved around the dial with silky smoothness rather than by little jerks.

I bought the SpaceView model with a transparent dial, and it is still my constant companion. Among other things, it reminds me to "always look for a *second* solution." That is, even when I find a solution for whatever problem, I look for a second one as well. (Bulova failed the test—they neglected to look into quartz movements as a "second solution." Within a few short years the Japanese, using quartz movements, ran over the Bulova folks like a steamroller.)

I still prefer the tuning-fork technology and am determined to wear my Accutron to the grave. Not long ago, when in Dallas on business, the battery in my watch went dead. Thinking there was "no problem," I had a new battery installed. Unknown to me, however, Bulova's 1.35-volt mercuric oxide low-drain battery had been outlawed in the U.S. because of its mercury content, and jewelers were substituting a different 1.5-volt battery. The result was that, two weeks later, half of the tuning fork's electronic circuit blew out. When I called the Bulova service department at 1-800-233-3350 in Woodside, New York, I was stunned to learn that they refuse to carry parts and repair Accutrons any longer. So where am I going with all this? *I found a solution with a repairman who is I-N-V-I-S-I-B-L-E!*

I started my search by calling jewelers in the Yellow Pages that listed "Bulova" as one of the brands they sold. The first three assured me that Bulova Accutrons could no longer be repaired, but the fourth jeweler was my kind of man. If I'd drop off the watch, he'd see to it that an independent repairman would fix it, and put in a new Eveready #387 1.35-volt mercuric oxide low-drain battery (at that time available in Canada).

"May I talk to the repairman, please?"

"No, he doesn't have any contact with the public."

At first I thought the jeweler was just trying to protect a commission, but further investigation proved this was not the primary reason. Whoever the repairman is, he deals only through established dealers, with all checks being made out to the jewelry store. And—listen to this!—the actual repairman has never been seen, and no one has a clue as to his name, address, or telephone number.

The only contact between the stores and the repairman is a courier known as Tony. Every Friday "Tony," who appears to be in his late seventies and walks with a limp, makes the rounds in this city, picking up and delivering Bulova Accutrons and similar models, receiving payment *in cash*. The store owners are happy because they get a commission and render a needed service to their customers, and we Bulova Accutron owners are happy to keep our watches running. Can this repair guy be tracked down? Without a subpoena, some industrial-strength threats, or a PI who successfully trails Tony, I don't think so. And who would want to? Why would anyone care?

Suppose, then, that you wish to set up an invisible, untraceable business and for whatever reason do not want to use a corporation, an LLC, nor a nominee. OK, why not copy the Bulova repairman?

1. Locate retail businesses or public offices where the owners are willing to act on your behalf in return for a commission. Contact them in person or via a representative. Your business could be in repair, replacement, software, small products, information, reports, or any other kind of business where *the customer would contact the store or office.*

2. Checks will be made out to your dealers, and the dealers will pay you or your rep in cash. They will want a receipt for their tax records, but this can be in any business name you like. Who cares; who would ever check?

3. You keep good records with QuickBooks (no audit trail when you correct errors), list the income on your personal tax return (Schedule C), and all's well with your world.

QUESTIONS & ANSWERS

What is a "fictitious" business name? Is it something fraudulent?

No, it has nothing to do with anything shady or illegal. State laws require any person who regularly transacts business for profit, in the state, under a "fictitious name" to register that business name with the Secretary of State's office. For a sole proprietorship or partnership, a business name is generally considered "fictitious" unless it contains the name of the owner or all of the general partners and does not suggest the existence of additional owners. Use of a name which includes words like "company," "associates," "brothers," or "sons," will suggest additional owners and will make it necessary for the business to file and publish the fictitious business name on company letterhead, business cards, in advertising, or on its product.

The problem with a fictitious name is that the owner of the business and the street address will be matters of public record. Although sometimes useful, I seldom recommend a fictitious name.

16

ANONYMOUS TRAVEL BY LAND, SEA, AND AIR

I want to be invisible . . . I paint my face and travel at night.

—Ralph Reed, as quoted in the *Virginian Pilot and Ledger Star*, 11/9/91

Airport surveillance is reaching extremes undreamed of in times gone by, making this the *least* anonymous way to travel. If, therefore, anonymity is your first concern, you may wish to travel by train, bus, or automobile. Nevertheless, most of us do travel by air, so let's tackle air travel first.

PURCHASING YOUR TICKET

Go to any length to avoid purchasing your ticket for cash at the airport. The person at the ticket counter will take your money but may secretly have you put under surveillance—in some airports the chances are fifty-fifty you will be stopped and questioned if you pay cash, especially for a one-way ticket. If you must pay cash, pay it to a travel agency beforehand. Better yet, pay the travel agent with a money order, or a check from your anonymous bank account.

SHOWING ID WHEN YOU CHECK IN

Use your passport rather than your driver's license because a passport does not show your address. And by the way, resist the temptation to try to avoid showing ID. In the summer of 1996, a prominent newsletter editor who "breathes, eats and sleeps privacy" (his own words) refused to show picture ID at Boston's Logan International Airport. When he informed the agent that the request was illegal, two security men were called in, and he was given a choice of either producing his driver's license or missing his flight.

"Since I absolutely positively *had* to be in Chicago that day no matter what," he said, "I produced it. These guys then photocopied it—and it had my Social Security number! Then they separated my luggage, searched and tagged it, and escorted me onto the plane. They passed the word to the cabin attendants, who then kept an eye on me the whole flight!"

USING YOUR OWN NAME

Remember when we used to travel under any name we chose, and traded, bought, and sold our tickets? You can still do that for national flights in most countries overseas, as well as in Canada and Mexico. No longer, however, in the United States. The so-called reason for this is that it keeps terrorists from traveling. I know of no travel agent that believes this. (After all, what self-respecting terrorist would not have fake ID?) The actual fact is that no one benefits other than:

The airlines. Unused nonrefundable tickets cannot be sold or transferred. Previously, if you purchased a ticket in advance, at a reduced fare, and then because of illness or a change in plans you decided not to go, you could sell the ticket to another person who would then fly in your name. Since you paid for the ticket, that was reasonable, was it not? But now, the airline keeps your money and sells the seat to someone else.

The government: An ominous trend in the United States over the past decade has been one of increased government surveillance over its noncriminal citizens. This includes the increasing demand for your Social Security number, the prohibitions against depositing or withdrawing large sums of cash from your bank account, the iron-handed regulations aimed at commercial mail receiving agencies, and the demand for your government-issued picture ID at the airport. I will not here speculate on the real reasons for this increasing control, nor will I comment on the claims others have made, that U.S. citizens now have less privacy than did German citizens in the 1930s. Let's be realists and see what can be done to lower our profiles.

You may decide that traveling under your own name is not a problem and does not compromise your privacy. Nevertheless, I suggest you immediately incorporate one small measure toward anonymity—purchase air tickets using just the initial of your first or middle name, plus your last name. Do not let your travel agent tell you this cannot be done. Thousands travel every day with tickets like J. Brown, R. Martin, and S. Smith. (One side benefit is that—if another family member has the same first or middle initial—he or she can use your ticket in case your plans change.)

USING A "MISSPELLED" NAME

This is an emergency method for the future, should you be fearful that someone is checking on your movements and may run a search via an air-travel database. In this case, *do* use your first name, and perhaps your middle name or initial as well. Change the first letter of your last name, thus throwing it into a completely different section of the alphabet. With this system, the true names on the left become "in error" the names on the right:

Rodgers ⇨	Dodgers	Russell ⇨	Mussell
Fox ⇨	Cox	Gardener ⇨	Dardener
Hall ⇨	Ball	Long ⇨	Fong
Perry ⇨	Gerry	Stockwell ⇨	Rockwell

As long as you are accurate with the first name and middle name or initial, you should not have a problem because you could always explain it as a "clerical error." This is especially true if you have an unusual name. Example: Your ticket name is Zenaida Z. Aadbadick and your real name is Zenaida Z. Zaabadick. (Naturally, you purchase your ticket at a travel agency where they do not know you.) Flash your passport at the airport counter. In actual practice, I have never found that anyone at the check-in counter even noticed the slight alteration.

Another ploy is to use an open ticket and show up at the last minute, thus avoiding the advance-registration computer database. If someone is trying to track you, by the time they have your flight data you will already have arrived at your destination and left the airport. However, if they are *really* after you, fly to an alternate airport. For example, if you are in Las Vegas and need to travel to Boston, fly to Chicago and catch a nonstop to Manchester, New Hampshire. Rent a car in Manchester and drive down to Boston.

DO NOT CHECK YOUR LUGGAGE

Sooner or later, something will be lost or stolen. Further, you want to be free to cancel at the last minute, switch to an earlier flight, or to another airline, or whatever. One of our sons-in-law travels the world for a manufacturing company, often away from home for weeks at a time. He dresses well because he meets with corporate CEOs, yet he has never once checked a suitcase.

(If you just can't live like that, then ship a case ahead via UPS or FedEx.)

FLYING WITH NO ID AT ALL

Since this system may be illegal, I was not going to mention it in this book. However, thinking about "Airport Insecurity" is making my blood pressure rise, so here we go. I am not suggesting *you* do the following but if ever my name and face show up sometime on the six o'clock network news, here is what *I* shall do:

1. I'll have a friend, or a college kid who needs some extra cash (they all do!), purchase a ticket in his own name to wherever I wish to go in the U.S., Canada, or Mexico. Or even back to the Canary Islands, if the friend/student has a passport to show. (On arrival in the Canaries, I will go through customs with my own passport.)

2. We'll go to the departure gate together and my confederate will show his ID and trade the ticket for a boarding card.

3. When the flight is called, I'll use that boarding card to board the plane. My accomplice leaves the airport, mission accomplished and his commission well earned. When I outlined this plan to my attorney, he said, "Man, will that ever complicate the insurance claim if your plane crashes!" Well, if the plane crashes, let the hotshot airline folks sort it out.

In fact, if time is of the essence, I may just go straight to the boarding area, pick out a sympathetic-looking type, give him or her a suitable sob story, and pay whatever it takes to get that boarding card.

Last-minute addition: United has secretly put in a system whereby a camera records the image of the "ticket purchaser" and the image appears on a small monitor at the departure gate. Therefore, avoid United and watch for this device on other airlines as well! It may be that you will have to find someone to buy your ticket that actually resembles you. However, the monitor is small and when passengers are streaming through, no close inspection will be made. Have your nominee wear the same jacket, hat, or sunglasses that you wear, when he steps up to the counter. Then take them back and wear them when boarding.

HOW TO MAINTAIN YOUR PRIVACY AT YOUR DESTINATION

You'll need transportation, a place to stay, and possibly a way to keep in touch with your bookie. Here are some tips:

Do not rent a car at the airport: Nor, if you can help it, anywhere else. Stick to taxis and limos, or borrow a car from a friend. At the very least, take the shuttle to your hotel and then check the yellow pages for some offbeat cheapo outfit that does not have a national 800 number. (The 800 number means they have a national database where you can easily be tracked.)

Name and address for registration at your motel: Note that I say motel, not hotel. In the past few years, most hotels have picked up a nasty habit of demanding picture ID. I recently flew into LA to attend Robert McKee's Story Seminar under an "alternate" name. However, when I tried to check into a hotel near the Pacific Design Center, the manager insisted on ID. I asked why.

"Well, maybe after you left, we found out a party had been held and your room was trashed."

"Do I look like the room-trashing type?"

"No, but you can never tell. One time it cost us more than $4,000 to repair the damage in a room."

"I can leave you a bank cashier's check for $5,000. That should put you at ease."

"Sorry, but no. We require picture ID."

Motels, however, are much less demanding. Give them an initial and a common last name, and any address you like. (When I travel in the USA and Canada I often use a mail-drop address in Spain, and when in Spain, a mail-drop address in Canada.)

Credit cards: Cash is preferable to a credit card. However, if you travel with a credit card, note that with some financial institutions—you can have two credit cards, one in your own name and a *second card in any other name you like.* If asked for a reason, tell them that you often travel under your professional name, since you are a writer, an entertainer . . . or (ahem) a foreign movie star.

Telephone calls: Never charge a call to your room. Use a prepaid telephone card (see Chapter 8). If you prefer a pay phone, keep in mind that some pay phones in certain luxury hotels (especially in Miami, Las Vegas, Houston, Los Angeles, and New York) are monitored. If you're spending a few days at Motel 6, however, not to worry about the pay phones.

Here is a better way, especially if you'll be staying for a week or more:

- Get a newspaper from your destination beforehand, and look up "Rooms for Rent" or "Roommates Wanted."
- Call ahead and arrange to see the room when you arrive.
- Explain that you hope to be there for about a year but, as something is pending, you'd like to take it for a provisional thirty days and will pay double if you can't stay longer. (Even so, you'll save money over a hotel room.)
- Arrange to have the temporary use of the landlord's or your roommate's telephone. Promise to place any long-distance calls on your phone card.

Anonymous travel is Level Three security. As long as you have taken the previous steps that keep your true name from ever being connected to your residence address, you may feel free to travel under your own first initial and last name. But if ever the time comes when you think you are being followed, then the information in this chapter may prove to be invaluable.

QUESTIONS & ANSWERS

Is it okay to travel by Amtrak?

Not if you value your privacy. Amtrak is worse than the airlines! They provide the DEA with ticketing information about passengers, including where they're coming from, where they're headed, whether they paid for their tickets with cash or credit and when they bought their tickets. A DEA official says, "Our agreement is that anything we seize off the train, Amtrak gets 10 percent."

My employer requires me to stay in five-star hotels under my own name. Any privacy tips?

Yes. If you have a notebook computer take every possible precaution. As I said in Chapter 3, a stolen notebook computer with corporate files can fetch up to $50,000. (And it is only a matter of time until Palm Pilots and other small computerized organizers will be targeted as well!) I suggest you take the following precautions:

1. Travel with a hard-side carry-on case such as one of the Samsonites that feature both a key lock and (more important) two combination locks. When you leave the room, lock your notebook computer inside.

2. Check out IBM's Smart Card Security Kit ($189). The Smart Card Reader installs in any Type II PC card slot and uses high-tech encryption and decryption. Data is encrypted and stored in the Smart Card's memory. The Smart Card's own processor handles all the security chores, so there's nothing to learn. Just plug it in and be safe. That way, even if the computer is stolen, the data will be safe from prying eyes.

3. For certain files that are especially sensitive, keep them *only* on a PC card with flash memory—the kind the new digital cameras use. This will be your D drive. I get my cards from SanDisk Corporation in Sunnyvale, California (408-542-0500), but many other companies make them as well. They are available in 20, 40, and 85MB capacities and are extremely easy to use. When you leave the room, just pop out the credit-card-sized disk and take it with you.

4. When you leave the room—whether you have a computer or not—leave the TV on and hang the Do Not Disturb card on the door. Schedule the maid's time to coincide with when you are there, or else tell the housekeeper to skip your room. (You can ask for clean towels anytime.)

5. Do not use the pay phones in the hotel for any sensitive calls. Find an alternate solution, such as using your cell phone away from the area.

6. If you are meeting someone clandestinely, keep in mind that there are many hidden surveillance cameras in these hotels, and they keep videotapes.

7. *No sensitive conversations in the elevator.* Many elevators in luxury hotels are bugged. If you wish to prove this, when going up alone, say to a make-believe companion, "OK, Bugsy, when Molly opens the door, shoot the broad right between her baby blue eyes!" Don't be surprised if met by the hotel's security forces when the elevator door opens. . . .

How can I make an anonymous overseas trip?

If you prefer to avoid U.S. Customs, first cross into Canada or Mexico, then book a round-trip flight from there. Even more private: book passage on a ship from either country. This should avoid having your name show up in a U.S. database. Further, you will be less likely to suffer the fate of the traveler whose case was discussed on "Eye on America," part of the CBS nightly news with Dan Rather on April 6, 1998.

Amanda, a fifty-four-year-old social worker who had been an American citizen for the past twenty years, took a trip to India. Upon her return to San Francisco, she was taken aside by U.S. Customs personnel and strip-searched. When nothing was found, she was x-rayed. When the x-ray showed nothing specific she was taken to a hospital and x-rayed again. Still nothing specific, so was she released? No. She was forced to take a powerful laxative that sent her to the toilet twenty-eight times, with agents present to examine the stools. Only when all results were negative was she released, *twenty-three hours later*, without an apology. As Dan Rather correctly pointed out, once you are in the clutches of Customs agents you lose almost all rights. No cause whatsoever is needed for a strip search, and you will not be allowed to call your lawyer, nor anyone else. Why was Amanda, carrying a U.S. passport, subjected to this treatment? Because she fit the so-called profile of a drug runner:

1. Her U.S. passport showed a foreign country as a place of birth,

2. She was a "woman traveling alone," and

3. She wore "bulky clothing."

My wife has flown between Spain and the United States a number of times, alone. Until now, nothing has happened, but the next time she plans to cross into Canada and fly over and back from there. We think the Canadians are a bit more civilized.

What if the police pull me over? I live in Illinois but drive with a Utah driver's license and the license plates are from Oregon.

Keep a suitcase in the trunk, an opened road map in the passenger seat, and a garment bag hanging from a hook over the left rear window. Your residence is in Utah (ghost address in West

Jordan Valley) but you work in Oregon. Currently you are on vacation. (It doesn't matter if your car is registered in the name of an LLC with an address in yet another state. Police seldom worry about the name a car is registered in as long as it's not stolen.)

Dress well, be polite, and don't drive more than five miles an hour over the limit. In addition, invest in a Valentine One radar/ laser detector. It has arrows to show from which direction you're being targeted.

Don't call attention to yourself with a vanity plate such as TOPSCRT, AU DGGER, or 90KPLUS. And by the way, there are several ways to avoid getting a ticket even if you *are* pulled over. One is to dress as a preacher or priest (or nun) and identify yourself as such. Another is to "break down and start crying," says Sergeant James M. Eagan, New York State Police (retired), author of *A Speeder's Guide to Avoiding Tickets*. Personally, I would prefer to pay the occasional ticket, but I pass this on as of possible interest to female readers, whether or not they are normally of the crying type.

Last summer, I admit to getting pulled over by a patrolman on U.S. 101, but I'd just reread Captain Robert L. Snow's book, *Protecting Your Life, Home, and Property* (mentioned previously). I looked the patrolman in the eye, said I knew I was guilty, treated him with respect, and offered no excuse. In his book, Snow says this has happened to him only two or three times in twenty-five years, and each time he was so flabbergasted he let the driver go with a "Please drive carefully." Snow was right. No ticket. I was merely told to "please drive carefully."

If a patrolman pulls me over for something minor like a taillight out, or an expired registration, can he search my car?

Legally no, unless a gun, alcohol, or drugs are *visible*. (However, if you are carrying a concealed weapon, inform the officer at once.)

Constantly check your lights and turn signals, and be *sure* the annual tag on your plates has not expired. (If you are *not* sure, stop reading and check the lights and license plate tag right now!) The justification for refusing to allow your car to be searched is a U.S. Supreme Court ruling, *Ohio v. Robinette* (No. 95-891), but the officer may intimidate you by saying "Please open your trunk," or "Would you open your glove compartment, please?" Tell him, in your *most respectful manner*, that your lawyer has told you never to allow a search of any kind without a warrant. The patrolman may search your car anyway, but whatever is seized may not be legal evidence if the case goes to court.

If I am a passenger in a car and a patrolman pulls over the driver, can the cop order me to step out of the car?

Until February 19, 1997, the answer was no. On that date, however, the U.S. Supreme Court, in a 7–2 decision, said yes, they can. In an Associated Press dispatch the next day, it was observed that, although officers may now order all passengers to step out of the car, the Supreme Court did not decide whether officers can bar passengers ordered out of a car from leaving the scene.

If I am a passenger, can the cop search my belongings without a warrant?

If your attorney is not up-to-date, he may think you cannot be searched. However, on April 5, 1999, there was a significant change in automobile search law. The U.S. Supreme Court (*Wyoming v. Houston* 119 SCt 1297) held that law-enforcement officers with probable cause to search a car may inspect passengers' belongings found in that car that are capable of concealing the object of the search.

"Passengers, no less than drivers, possess a reduced expectation of privacy with regard to the property that they transport in cars." (119 S Ct at 1298.)

In other words, if the cop suspects that the *driver* has contraband of any kind, he may also search the purses, briefcases, suitcases, etc. of the passengers, even if he has no reason to believe that they are guilty of anything whatsoever. Warn your friends to be careful with whom they ride . . . and take care yourself.

Can the police demand my Social Security number?

It depends on the state and whether the cop is having a good day. One of my readers (Vic) was caught doing fifty in a thirty-mile speed zone in Bellevue, Washington. The car, with Washington plates, was registered in the name of an LLC with a Cheyenne, Wyoming address. His driver's license is from another state that does not require a Social Security number.

"Where do you live?" asked the cop. Vic gave the address on his driver's license.

"Do you work for this company in Wyoming?" No, said Vic, he owned it. And then came the crunch, as the cop was writing out the ticket:

"And your Social Security number?"

"With all due respect, Officer, I do not give my Social Security number to *anyone.*"

"That may be the case in your state, but here in Washington we track all traffic fines with Social Security numbers. May I have your number, sir?"

"I never give this number out. Does Washington state law *require* the number?"

"Our policy [note: he didn't say law] is to list all Social Security numbers on traffic tickets."

"If it is not the law," he said in his most humble voice, "then I regret to say that I cannot give my Social Security number, Officer."

After a pause, the cop said to sign the ticket. Vic signed, was given a copy, and sped on his way. The box for the Social Security number was left blank. But note the question that follows:

Does it make any difference if I talk back to a police officer?

An article in the April 26, 1998, *Seattle Times* was headlined "MAN ARRESTED, HANDCUFFED FOR LACKING LITTER BAG." It starts out, "A motorist stopped for speeding was arrested and handcuffed by Olympia police officers for failing to have a litter bag in his car." The arresting officer made it clear that "not just any litter bag would do," insisting that the motorist was required to carry a "state-approved and-designed litter bag." (State officials, however, admit that such bags are no longer made.) The motorist was then hauled off, handcuffed, to the city jail.

Three months later, the *National Enquirer* ran a similar headline, "HANDCUFFED AND JAILED—FOR NOT HAVING A LITTER BAG IN HIS CAR." The *Enquirer* article, however, left out a vital detail. The original article in the *Times* explains why the unlucky motorist was *really* arrested:

[The motorist] acknowledges mouthing off to the officers.

So then, if you don't want your privacy invaded by seeing your name in the papers and in a national tabloid, it might be prudent not to "mouth off" to a police officer.

If we leave on a long trip, should we leave a key with a neighbor?

Not only would I not leave a key—I would not even tell the neighbor we were leaving. (Our homes always have complex timers that turn on lights, TV, stereo, sprinklers, etc. at varying times.) Louis R. Mizell, Jr., in his book *Invasion of Privacy*, tells the story of a Maryland couple who, before leaving on a vacation in August 1994, left a key with a neighbor. When they returned from their trip they picked up the key, thanked the neighbor, and thought no more about it.

"Then," writes Mizell, "in January 1995, the couple was adjusting a heating vent in their bathroom when they discovered a camera. Later that night, the couple found a second camera behind a heating vent in a dressing room and followed cables leading through their attic, down a drainpipe and underground into their neighbor's home. The neighbor had been watching the couple in the bathroom and dressing room for months—and it wasn't against the law."

We rent an apartment, and although we never leave a key with anyone when going on vacation, the landlord does have a key. How can we protect ourselves?

Landlords surreptitiously enter apartments more often than you might think—in fact, it once happened to me. That was forty-five years ago, but there were such serious consequences that I haven't forgotten it yet. Anthony Herbert, in his book *Complete Security Handbook*, has this to say in the section about locks:

- Change them without the management's knowledge. Remove the cylinder, take it to a locksmith, and get combination changed. If manager or janitor later complains, ask why he was attempting to enter your apartment while you were not present. (Better to incur a minor lease violation than to be dead!)
- No one should be permitted to visit your apartment unaccompanied, except in a life-and-death emergency!

17

COMPUTERS, E-MAIL, AND THE INTERNET

It is easier to get into the enemy's toils than out again.
—THE LION, THE FOX AND THE BEASTS
(AESOP)

"When you belly up to your keyboard to trade notes with a colleague," writes Eryn Brown in an article in *Fortune*, "you may feel you're in a cozy conversation. Legally and technologically, however, you are as exposed as dummies in a department-store window. Note well: If your computer belongs to the company, so does its content. The law lets bosses read what you put there, and because of the herd-of-elephants memory capacity of modern systems, there's rarely a keystroke a suspicious or vengeful boss can't drag up."

The author is right. "Deleted" e-mail, like the Energizer Bunny, just keeps going and going and going. This is because many networks routinely store backups of *all* mail that passes through them. Security is no better when it comes to your home computer, or to your travels on the Internet. This danger was emphasized a few years ago in a *Wall Street Journal* article, "Internet Users, Better Beware: There Are Prying Eyes Online":

> While you sign on to the Internet and blithely zap and receive electronic mail, visit Web sites and bare your soul in on-line discussion groups, you are increasingly being watched and tracked. . . . Information about you is already on the Internet for millions of eyes to see.

YOUR HOME COMPUTER

If you already have a computer, and have not previously been security-conscious, then your name is almost certainly inside your computer somewhere. When you are connected to the outside world, remember that this is not a one-way street. Electronic traffic moves in both directions. Even when not connected, you may get a surprise when installing new software and your name shows up as the user even though you hadn't typed it in.

Therefore, if you already have a computer, your name is probably already in it, along with your address, your telephone number, and other personal details from your computer. To purge this information you must go into the registry—a delicate process indeed—so if you're not 100 percent sure you can do it, call in professional help.

If you've purchased a used computer, the seller may think he cleaned up the files, but his name will most likely still be embedded somewhere. If you want to leave it in, fine, but make certain you haven't also entered your own name when installing additional software.

When you purchase a computer in the future, do not, under any circumstances whatsoever, fill in your own name, address, telephone number, or any other personal data. If the computer will not start up, or the software will not load, until you fill in the blanks, put in something like Bob or Suzy, with a fake address in Canada or Europe. If a telephone number *must* be entered, use 555 after the area code, as this number will not belong to anyone. Example: 307-555-1234. Only after your computer has been certified as squeaky-clean should you consider connecting to the Internet.

NOTHING ON YOUR HARD DRIVE IS SECURE

When you delete a file, you actually delete only the address. The file itself remains on your hard drive. Although there are many programs that purport to erase the entire file by writing over it, they are not secure if the government is after you. You can even reformat your hard drive and the information may still be on there.

Bruce Schneier, author of *E-mail Security*, says, "The only secure computer is one that's turned off, locked in a safe, and buried 20 feet down in a secret location—and I'm not completely confident of that one either."

When I purchase a new computer, I take the hard drive out of the old one and literally smash it to pieces with a hammer.

NOTHING ON YOUR RECORDABLE CD-ROM IS SECURE

An article in the *Wall Street Journal* titled "It Slices, It Dices, It Disintegrates Digital Data" discusses the Secured Engineered Machinery Co. "They manufacture a machine about the size of a microwave . . ." that literally power-buffs data off CD-ROMS and turns the surface material of the disks into a fine plastic dust.

This machine sells—and is selling briskly—for $5,100. Why not just break up the disk? To quote from the article, ". . . even a fragment of carelessly discarded plastic or silicon might yield many paragraphs of text . . . even burning the materials could produce ash particles still large enough to produce data."

NOTHING ON THE INTERNET IS SECURE

There is no such thing as electronic security if a modem is involved. Sad news, but better to learn this now than later.

True, a message itself, when sent over the Internet, can be encrypted with Pretty Good Privacy (PGP), and perhaps the keys can be successfully hidden, but the *senders and receivers can be identified*, as even superhacker Kevin Mitnick learned to his sorrow. I recently had a chat with Michael Paciello, author of *WEBable* and an international consultant on Internet privacy. For more than two hours I fired questions at him about making e-mail more private. "What about a fictitious name on Juno? What about PGP encryption? What about putting e-mail on disks and sending them out at Cybersmith? Or with a phone card? Or mailing the disk to London for resending?"

"Jack," he answered, "Nothing you've suggested is secure, as far as hiding who sends the message and who receives it. Given the time and the motive, backed up with enough expense money, I'll trace you down every single time!"

ANONYMOUS REMAILERS

If you wish to send an e-mail to someone and hide the fact it came from you, you might send it to a remailer. This is a service using a computer that will strip away your old identity, give you a new one, and then send your e-mail to its final destination. There are many popular remailers, although some have a short life.

A *psuedo anonymous remailer* will know your actual e-mail address. This means that someone could get a court order to force the remailer operator to reveal this address.

An *anonymous remailer* is more secure. Nobody, not even the remail service, knows who you are. Also, an anonymous remail can be sent via a string of remailers—otherwise known as chain remail—making it even more secure. However, this is quite complicated and for that reason seldom used. I do not use remailers because:

1. It is almost a certainty some of these remailers are sting operations run by a government. They are specifically designed to trap you.

2. There is a PI who runs seminars for other PIs, teaching them how to track down those that send anonymous e-mails. (I sent him an e-mail asking for details and received this reply: "Why would I want to give information to someone writing a book about how to hide assets and identities, when that is the very thing that I investigate? Don't you think it would be rather stupid of me . . . ?"

3. Unknown to the remailer's administrator hackers can and do break into these systems. They can then read and copy messages at will. (In one well-known case, an unknown hacker worked out a method to send messages via a remailer in such a way that if the recipient answered in a similar fashion, his true e-mail name and address would be instantly captured!)

4. Some believe—and I am one of them—that the U.S. government collects, scans, and stores all messages—including passcodes—that go into and out from the remailers.

E-MAIL TIPS

If by any chance you have Juno, get rid of it at once—it is riddled with security holes. Hotmail also has some problems, especially in the heading. At the present time, hushmail is my favorite. Go to www.hushmail.com to learn more about it and to sign up. Do not, of course, enter any information that will reveal your true identity.

If you wish to purchase something on the Internet and are in doubt about the security of sending your credit card number, send part of your credit card number in one e-mail, and the balance of the number in a second e-mail. It is very unlikely that anyone will come across both e-mails in a random search.

In earlier times, viruses came in the form of attachments and as long as you didn't open any strange attachments, all was well. Now, however, some viruses come in the subject line and attack as soon as you click on the message to read it. If you are using Outlook Express, here is the solution: Go to View and the Layout. Under "Preview Pane", uncheck the box that says "Show Preview Pane." Now your email messages will not come up without a double click. If, therefore, you see an incoming message that is from a suspicious source, give it a single click to highlight it. Then delete it.

If you have access to *PC WORLD*, check the May 2001 special issue dedicated to more privacy on the Internet. On page 98, e-mail problems are discussed. For details about the problems—and the ways to correct some of them, go to www.privacyfoundation.org/resources/javascriptoff.asp#outlook5.

STEGANOGRAPHY

"Steganography" refers to the sending of a picture with a hidden text file inside the picture. Even if intercepted, there is no outward clue that a message is hidden inside, yet with a special program it pops out effortlessly. A password is used, known to both the sender and receiver, so even if the bad guys check all images with the hidden message program they must still break out the password. At one time I started using steganography, but since the other party has to have the same software program—and use it as well—it didn't work out. The software program I was using for hidden images at that time was *S-Tools*, available on the Internet. However, changes are so rapid in this field that I suggest you search the Net yourself for the latest information on "Steganography." (Be careful to spell it as shown, and not as "stenography.")

THE BOTTOM LINE FOR SENDING A SECRET MESSAGE

Assume anything you say in an e-mail will be read by others. An e-mail message may linger on backup tapes for years on end—then come back to haunt you. (They are increasingly being used in civil and criminal cases.) Teach your children that a silly or profane e-mail in their youth could come back to bite them years later.

If you or anyone in your family has a truly confidential message to send, do as I do. Seal it in an envelope, stamp it, and mail it.

QUESTIONS & ANSWERS

If I never use my computer at work for e-mail, will I have a reasonable amount of privacy?

You still have to be careful what you type. A new generation of software is emerging to permit employers to record not just which Web sites employees browse, but also which programs they use, memos they write, e-mail they send—in short, every keystroke. Win What Where, a software company in Kennewick, Washington, released its entrant into the field in 1999, a program which costs $285 for each desktop computer in which it is installed. The company says its software keeps a record of every keystroke, mouse click, and command.

Another company, Tech Assist of Largo, Florida, began distributing Desktop Surveillance in North America, a comprehensive computer-monitoring program by the British company Omniquad. The software costs $55 per computer and has been on sale in Europe for about a year and a half. Desktop Surveillance is being marketed as the "software equivalent of a video surveillance camera on the desktop." It permits third-party observers to view, in real time or in playback, exactly what tasks a user is performing and what keystrokes he or she is entering.

Each of the foregoing programs lets employers hide the fact that the software is running on an employee's computer. Desktop Surveillance even allows a record of the employee's activities to be e-mailed to a supervisor without an employee's knowledge.

Officials from both Tech Assist and Win What Where said they saw a demand from employers concerned about employees wasting time on their computers. They also said that employers wanted a record in case the employees sued or were sued.

Is it safe to keep secret files on my home computer, as long as they are encrypted?

If your home is ever searched, count on your computer being hauled away. And when put to the test, it will almost certainly talk. Many programs, such as Microsoft Word or Lotus 1-2-3, make *temporary* copies that may linger on. Is there no solution? Well, not if the location of your computer is known. So do not let it be known! If you work at home, no one besides your close friends and (perhaps) relatives should know where you live. If the investigators cannot find you, they cannot confiscate your computer. If you fear surreptitious entry when you are away from home, here are two suggestions:

- Use a notebook computer only, and take it with you when you leave, or
- Use a computer with a removable hard drive and take the hard drive with you when you leave.

Here is something else to worry about—just in case you and your spouse are not getting along. There are many companies that offer to snoop into any computer you bring them. Prices range from $150 to $250 an hour, and they seldom fail to bring up supposedly secret files. In one recent nasty divorce case, the wife suspected her husband was not declaring all his savings or investments. She hired a computer snoop to search her husband's computer. Bingo! Up came a record of his inquiries to an on-line service. He had been using it to track his unreported stocks. If you still have confidence in your exotic encryption system, consider this. If a lawsuit is filed and you are deposed, you will be asked under oath to explain *why* you have encrypted these files.

18

CROSSING THE CANADIAN AND MEXICAN BORDERS

Fear of jail is the beginning of wisdom.

—SEEN ON A BRIGHTLY PAINTED CHAMBER POT IN NIGERIA

As you have seen in previous chapters, there is seldom any reason to leave the country merely to protect your privacy. Nevertheless, situations may arise that indicate a temporary journey to Mexico or Canada.

From the United States you can easily cross into Canada or Mexico—legally or illegally. Legally is better. Use your passport for ID since it has less information than a driver's license, and—unlike when making a trip to other foreign countries, it will not be stamped to show entry or exit. These two countries are thus ideal for those of you who may need emergency asylum and/or to keep a few assets out of the country, should the floodgates of heaven ever open to rain disaster down upon your U.S.A. parade. If this is of interest, I suggest you practice crossing the borders both north and south. Don't make a special trip; just work it into vacation time or perhaps incorporate it into a tax-deductible business trip. If you are a U.S. citizen there should be no problem either entering or leaving, and that must be your goal. *No problems.*

I say that because there are two types of border inspections, primary and secondary. You do not want secondary, not ever, because then your name will go into the computer and, to paraphrase the ads for the Roach Motel, travelers who check *in* to the computer never check out. Here then are some random comments:

- Dress like a tourist. Clean and neat but no tie.

- Do not cross with anything to declare, or with any item even remotely suspicious. No fruit, no weapons, no drugs. Best way to cross is on a tour bus. Next best way is on foot, at a busy crossing, during the busiest hours, but taking a car is certainly more convenient, despite the fact its license plate number may go into a computer.

- Do not cross into Mexico with an RV if you can avoid it. Some Americans have been arrested in Mexico and held under false pretenses, with the goal of allowing the American to go free if he leaves his motor home behind. (An RV is OK for Canada, but radar detectors are not, so leave your fuzzbuster behind you.)

- If there are several lines leading to multiple booths at the crossing, pick your lane and then stick with it. If you change lanes, the inspector from the original lane may spot you, think you're trying to avoid him, and make you get back in line. Then, when your turn comes, you'll get more attention than you really wanted to receive.

Never cross in either direction with a bad attitude, as I did one August day in 1995, returning from Mexicali when it was 112 degrees in the shade and there was no shade. The result was that the U.S. Immigration and Naturalization inspector started searching the car I was driving (which was in another name, and me without backup documentation!). Fortunately, when going through the trunk he opened my briefcase and found a well-worn Bible I usually carry with me. At this point I loosened up, forced the hint of a smile, and said it was always nice to talk to folks about the Scriptures. That's probably all that saved me from the dreaded secondary inspection. The inspector snapped my brief-case shut, dropped the trunk lid, and waved me on through. Relieved, I stopped down the road at Pepe's Cantina in Calexico for two chilled bottles of Miller's Genuine Draft.

Do you think a policeman, a highway patrolman, or an FBI agent has power? *You ain't seen power till you've met the U.S. border inspector.* Any kind of trouble, and you will be considered guilty until you can prove yourself innocent.

Incidentally, never call an inspector working for the Immigra-tion and Naturalization Service (INS) a "Customs" official, nor let him hear the phrase from your lips, "going through Customs" (even though that's what I call it myself, as a general term in this report). There are two agencies at the border, U.S. Customs and the INS, and I'm here to tell you they do not get along well with one another. (INS deals with people, Customs deals with goods, but their duties overlap.) You don't have to tell them apart, just don't address them by any title whatsoever. Instead, stick to "Sir" or "Ma'am."

Men, go through your billfolds and ladies, examine your purses. Both Customs inspectors (CIs) and immigration inspec-tors (IIs) can treat you and your passengers like pieces of meat to be inspected. No, they are normally not out to get you, but we all have an off day once in a while—such as the day I returned from Mexicali—and these folks have awesome authority, no search warrants needed.

If they ask you for your billfold, hand it over. If they ask you to open every box and suitcase, open them. If they want to check the oil in your NorthStar engine, hand them your last Kleenex to wipe the dipstick. Burn this into your brain: Never say to the inspector, "You can't touch that!" The inspector certainly can. *And will!*

So if you're Senior Senator Sam from Sacramento, traveling with Sweet Suzy Secretary, either drop those condoms before you get to the border or be prepared to stifle your embarrassment. (Condoms are not, of course, illegal.) Both CIs and IIs can ask you any question, no matter how embarrassing or insulting, and they expect an answer:

"Is this young lady *really* your wife?"

"How much money do you make a year?"

"Ever been arrested for smuggling? How about rape?"

Lawyers (and some egocentric businessmen) will respond, "Do I have to answer that?" And the response, as given by ex–Immigration inspector Ned Beaumont in his book *Beat the Border,* is:

> You don't have to answer. But then again, you don't have to cross the border. And you're not going to cross the border until you answer that question and *any others I see fit to ask.* Understand?

CIs and IIs are skilled at deception, a.k.a. lying. If they preface something by saying "You don't need to worry about thus-and-so . . ." *start worrying!* They may try the good cop/bad cop routine, like in the movies. Remember that it's really bad cop/worse cop. These folks are not your buddies. Keep cool and collected on the outside, skeptical and cynical on the inside.

Leaving the United States is easy, especially when crossing the southern border at a busy location. It's the return trip to watch out for, and a final word of warning here: Don't try using a false ID. Even if it's perfect, *you'll* know it's not, and they'll sense that fact. Beaumont makes this point at great length in *Beat the Border*, and I can do no better than to quote a very small part of his "People Smarts" section:

> Inspectors, by the very nature of their job, become "people smart" very quickly. . . . They turn into masters of reading people. The chief people-smart skill an inspector develops is the ability to tell when someone is lying. An inspector's ability to spot a liar becomes a kind of instinct, or sixth sense. He may not always be able to fully analyze or explain why he knows someone is lying, but the inspector knows it nonetheless. He knows with a certainty that's inexplicable but real. . . . All inspectors develop the same instincts. If there's one genuine skill I've retained from my days on the line, it's the ability to spot a lie.

The author then lists examples of others skilled at their craft, such as an auto mechanic who can diagnose an engine's faults just by listening to it run. He reminds the reader of the inspector's job, how he questions hundreds of people a day, six days a week, week after week.

> An inspector talks to more liars in a month than the layman does in a lifetime. How good at spotting liars do you think that inspector is going to be in a year? Or five? Or ten? I've worked with inspectors who'd been on the job for 20 years. They could detect a lie . . . *without fail*, in the first five seconds of the inspection.

Now that I've done my best to scare you, let me put your mind at ease. When you are reentering the United States, the inspector's first question will be something like "Of what country are you a citizen?" You answer "U.S.A.," and he may ask the town or county where you were born. Assuming you do remember that and answer honestly, you're just about home and should have no problems.

Nevertheless, a review of this section will do no harm. What occasionally happens is that the inspector gets bored. To break this boredom-at-the-border syndrome, he may vary his questions from time to time. In addition to the ones mentioned earlier, he might ask, watching your eyes to see if you lie:

"What were you doing in Toronto, Miss Curvilinear?"

"What do you have to declare, Dr. Shepherd?"

"How long have you been out of the United States, Judge Joseph Force Crater?"

"What was the purpose of your trip to Tijuana, Counselor?"

In this case, don't just answer "business" or "pleasure"—the inspectors hear that all the time. If it was pleasure, be specific, as in "I went to see my girlfriend who works with the PRI." Or if it was legal business, it's OK to say, "I've got a case about a Mexican trademark and I interviewed a guy at Lechuga, Zanahoria & Batata." The inspector doesn't care if you're bribing one of LZ&B's clerks to spill secrets, he's just watching to see if you're telling the truth.

"What do you do for a living, Dr. Jekyll?"

Oh-oh, here is where the rubber may meet the road. If your job is marrying old ladies for their money and then changing their medicine, it's time for:

ILLEGAL BORDER CROSSINGS

Hopefully you will never be in such danger that you will have to think about making an illegal crossing and again, I don't recommend that you break the law. But why not at least briefly consider what is involved?

CANADA

There are many unmanned areas along the border between the United States and Canada. My favorite is along the northern border of Minnesota. When you look at a map, you will see that Highway 11 follows the south side of the Rainy River from International Falls to Baudette. On the Ontario side, Canadian Highway 11 follows the same river on the northern side. It *appears* that you could just drop a raft in the river and paddle across. Don't be deceived by appearances. Homes line both sides of this wide river and there are informers on both sides. The border patrol catches persons on a regular basis there, with small fast boats that appear out of nowhere.

Instead, if you are in Baudette in the summer or fall, drive north to Lake of the Woods. This is hundred-mile-wide lake that spans the border. Rent a fast boat at one of the many resorts and buy a chart of the lake. Leave before dawn (when the lake is at its calmest) and go north for nine miles. Then cut to starboard, crossing the invisible boundary, and make your way east between Big Island and Bigsby Island. Your destination is beautiful Nestor Falls, on Highway 71.

Let's say you have an accomplice named Bud. Each of you will carry a VHF-FM radio. Bud will drive a car across the bridge from Baudette to the village of Rainy River, Ontario. Going through Customs here takes about forty-five seconds. He will drive thirty-four miles east to Highway 71, then go north exactly 33.8 miles to the small bridge that crosses Nestor Falls just beyond Helliar's resort. The narrow highway curves around a corner and Bud can stop at the wide turnout on his left, which borders Lake of the Woods. It is directly opposite a blue-and-white sign that says ONTARIO: Sunset Grove Camp.

A tiny twelve-by-twelve-foot vacant cabin sits down toward the water. Bud goes down the twenty-two steps (painted with blue trim that is fading) and on to a seven-by-fourteen-foot wooden dock. When he looks around, he will see that this dock is hidden from view in both directions. He calls you on the radio to say he is ready when you are. As you approach the Nestor Falls area by boat, you will see a tall radio tower to your left. Turn left, then right, into the small bay. You will see Bud standing on the dock.

I last ran this—I mean, I was last in the area in the fall of 1999. The old cabin and the dock were still there. There are no border-patrol boats this far north of the border, and no Customs checkpoints between Rainy River and Kenora, far to the northwest. There is considerable boat traffic between Nestor Falls and the Minnesota side in the summer, as well as snowmobile traffic in the winter. The locals on both sides merely obtain a yearly pass. Believe it or not, there is an honor system here. When they make a run in either direction they just call Customs and tell them who they are and where they are going.

MEXICO

There is no honor system along the southern border. Worse, what appears to be the "obvious" way—contacting a "coyote" and paying them the current price of $1,500, is the worst way of all—a gringo stands a good chance of getting either ripped off or killed outright.

Instead, take Highway 94 from San Diego and go through Jamul and Dulzura to American Tecate, at the border. Tecate, BCN, is a small city built around a typical Spanish plaza, whereas its California namesake is just a wide spot in the road, so the locals distinguish the two by calling the California one Tecatito ("Little Tecate").

After looking over the border crossing into Tecate, BCN to get a feel for the area, backtrack down Highway 94 six miles, slip on your pack, and head into the forest with compass and wire clippers. As long as you head northwest you'll be OK— pretty hard to miss Mexico! Allow five hours (it's a steep uphill climb), take plenty of water, and plan to arrive just before dark. You'll come to a poorly maintained wire fence and there will be humble hovels on the far side. Clip on through after dark, or climb over, or just follow the fence west until it ends in the forest. There is no Mexican border patrol to keep gringos out. *Nada.*

Tecate is a very nice place, in a high mountain valley with excellent cool and sunny weather, *simpático* people, and less crime than elsewhere along the border. Take a tour of the Tecate *cerveza* factory before you press on.

QUESTIONS & ANSWERS

If coyotes are to be avoided at all costs, how can I cross back into the U.S. undetected?

I posed this question to a friendly border guard, and this is his word-for-word reply:

"If he's a U.S.C. [U.S. citizen], I'd say walk across the border at a busy time at a legal POE [Point of Entry]. It's unlikely he'll get sent to secondary/delayed/caught/etc. as long as he dresses to fit in, is polite, doesn't fit any obvious profile, and has a legit-sounding story."

How about crossing into Canada north of Seattle, to the east of I-95?

You mean up by Blaine, on the way to Vancouver, BC? True, about half of the U.S. Border Patrol agents at Blaine were transferred to San Diego two years ago. When that happened, a number of persons incorrectly assumed that illegal crossings would be easier. Not so—the remaining agents know most of the "secret" crossings. They have installed remote-control cameras in some sections, and seismic sensors in others.

How about crossing into Canada through one of the Indian reservations along the border?

Actually, that's not a bad idea as long as you don't try to sneak through on your own. The reservation borders are tightly controlled by the Indian Mafia, sometimes in collaboration with the real Mafia. They can get you across safely for a reasonable fee. The trick is to contact them. I have no magic formula, but there are often casinos on the reservations, and if so, that is the place to start.

Is it OK to apply for a tax refund on Canadian purchases, when returning to the States?

We used to stop at one of those "duty-free" stores on the Canadian side, turn in receipts there for hotel, major purchases, etc. and get a cash refund on some of the taxes. We no longer do this, however, because—since February 1, 1999—to get a refund you must give them your name, address, telephone number, driver's license number, and the license-plate number of the car you are driving. *Your driver's license will be photocopied.* (The reason they give me for this is "increased fraud.")

Is there any special precaution to take, for a day-trip into Tijuana by car?

Yes. Buy one-day auto insurance as soon as you cross the border. (There are shops along the way with signs.) Tijuana's police (totally corrupt) are making routine stops to see if American drivers have Mexican insurance. If you have purchased this insurance, show them your receipt and you will be on your way. Otherwise, you will be offered a "choice": pay a stiff bribe on the spot or spend a few hours in jail. [Take it from this writer, you'd rather pay the bribe.]

How does the U.S. Border Patrol pick and choose at the checkpoint?

This question was asked by a reader of the *Los Angeles Times*. He said he passed the San Clemente border checkpoint nearly every day, and was almost always waved through. However, one day he noticed a Border Control officer taking a closer look at his car so he stopped to ask what he was looking at. The officer said he was checking to see if the car was riding low. The reader asked David Haldane, a staff writer at the *Times*, why he was almost invariably waved through when others were sometimes stopped. Also, why would the officer care if his car rode low, or not?

Haldane referred the question to Roy Villareal, a spokesman for the U.S. Border Patrol in San Diego. Villareal suggested that if the reader was not stopped, it might be that he was a "regular" who was recognized by the guards. Another reason might be that he did not display any of the suspicious behaviors the border patrol looks for.

What they look for is a visible increase in uneasiness as the officer approaches, and if they spot it, they will stop the driver for that reason alone.

"The first thing that comes out of the officer's mouth" said Villareal, is "good morning," or "good afternoon," and, at that instant, the subjects level of nervousness escalates from zero to 100. "You can see the arteries in their neck pulsing, or they will start sweating even in the dead of winter. Sometimes you say good morning, and they can't even answer you." At that point, of course, the officer will search the car.

As for looking at how the car rides, the purpose is to see if there is an unusal weight aboard. If the front end of the car is high but the rear end is close to the ground, the car will be stopped and the trunk opened.

What is the best way to send mail to Mexico?

Mail service south of the border is a disaster. Mailmen are underpaid, undersupervised, and some can just barely read. If a letter does not "look important," they may do one of two things: throw it away immediately or set it aside to deliver "mañana." In Spain, the word mañana usually means "tomorrow." In Mexico, however, it merely indicates "not today." Tomorrow may never come. There is no best way to send mail there but here is the least worst way. I learned this from a mailman in Ameca, Jalisco and I have tested it many times. The letter must *look* important. If you plan to receive mail in Mexico, give the following suggestions to the sender in the U.S.:

1. Use a business-size (#10) envelope. Smaller ones seem to get lost, and larger envelopes do not fit well into the mail pouch.

2. Type the address, or print it on a laser printer in large, easy-to-read letters. I use sixteen-point bold.

3. Put a return address on the reverse side of the envelope. Make it look important, such as putting "Dr." in front of your name, or perhaps a religious title. *Obispo* (bishop) is even better.

4. Put small-denomination postage stamps across the entire top of the envelope, to make the envelope look impressive. A well-to-do Mexican friend of mine in Reno, Nevada, puts half a dozen first-class commemorative stamps on every letter he mails to his relatives in Cabo San Lucas, but I have a better way. I purchase old stamps from Joe Kenton, PO Box 480456, Kansas City, MO 64148-0456. Like many other dealers, he sells old stamps—some of them dating back to when first-class postage was three cents—at a ten-percent discount off face value. In addition to saving money, the old stamps are real attention-getters.

5. Use some sort of rubber stamp near the left border, to give the impression that this is a registered or certified letter. I use three stamps and three ink pad colors on my letters. First, the outline of the U.S. eagle in red. Then a box with dotted borders and the word "FILED" above it. This is in blue. Last comes the date stamp (black), inserted into the box with the border.

About 95 percent of such letters get through—quite a record for south of the border!

19

SECRET HIDING PLACES

The young man knows the rules, but the old man knows the exceptions.

—ANONYMOUS

Don't laugh when I tell you this, but after hiding it, be sure you can someday still *remember* wherever it was you hid the machine pistols/ammunition/jewelry and precious stones/chemical products; clippings/videos/photographs/gold coins/silver dollars/negotiable securities/secret maps/compromising documents/forbidden books/red-hot love letters/Canadian $1,000 bills/whatever.

From 1959 until General Franco ordered Spain's laws to be changed in 1970, my companions and I were hiding small boxes in all of Spain's fifty provinces, and with the advent of legality, a plaintive cry was heard across the land: *"I can't remember all the places where I hid things!"*

And now, with that warning out of the way, let's discuss how you can hide items of varying sizes and values. Here are the categories:

Small: Valuable stamps, bills, gold coins (scattered in various locations), diamonds, and other items up to the size of a miniature pistol.

Medium: Documents, books, stacks of letters, and guns up to the size of a rifle.

Large: From computers and file cabinets up to you yourself, your mate, your mother, or your mistress.

In your home: With one exception (a secret alcove which I'll mention later), do not hide anything in the master bedroom. Burglars, sneaky visitors, police, private investigators, U.S. marshals, the DEA, and members of the Bureau of Alcohol, Tobacco and Firearms (ATF) will look there first. Here are a few suggestions for hiding small items in your home or yard:

- Interior of hollow doors, or inside rolled-up window shades.
- Inside a doghouse or a rabbit hutch, or in the crawl space under the house.
- Under the insulation in the attic (one of my favorites).
- Behind wall phones or cold air return vents.
- In the bottom of dog food or kitty litter bag.
- In the bottom half of a double boiler, or a box of sanitary napkins.
- Inside zippered cushions, hollow canes, or umbrellas.
- Inside a guitar or other musical instrument, or in the empty case of an old portable radio.
- In file cabinets (with innocuous file names).
- Inside an old stereo or TV set in the garage.

If you are handy with tools, you might build your own secret compartments. In *The Big Book of Secret Hiding Places*, by Jack Luger (Loompanics Unlimited, 1987), plans are given for building secret spaces under bottom drawers, inside upholstered furniture, behind medicine cabinets, and under stairs. There are also sections on hiding places on your person, in your yard, or in your motor vehicle.

In any of our various homes, it would seem to be no problem to leave cash and other valuables out in plain view. After all, the addresses are secret, and if the bad guys *can't find* the house they can't raid it! However, I do keep valuables well hidden and so should you. Can you guess why?

Correct! If a burglar is attracted to your home, it doesn't matter what arrangements have been made for privacy because it's not *you* he's after, it's the house. Since you will never know where I live, and assuming any burglar making a random strike will not have read this book, I feel confident in telling you some of the ways I hide small, medium, and large items in one home or another:

Small: Since I'm a great believer in having cash available for emergency use, I keep old junk-mail envelopes with pesetas, pounds, deutsch marks or dollars in:

- Sheet music in my wife's piano bench.
- In a box of old tax receipts in a storage unit.
- In the book *Using Microsoft Word 97*, one of more than eight hundred business and computer books in my library.
- In *History of the Guanches*, one of the six-hundred-plus hanging files in the storage cabinets of my home office, and
- Rolled up and inserted into a "foot powder" spray can with a removable bottom. I purchased this via mail order and keep it in my carry-on case when traveling.

When my car was stolen from SeaTac airport, the thieves broke open the glove compartment searching, I assume, for a gun. All they found were stacks of what appeared to be junk mail, so they tossed all those envelopes on the floor and the envelopes were still there when the police recovered the car. The *police* didn't notice, *either*, that two of those so-called junk mail envelopes had five $50 bills in each.

*   *   *

When I travel, I use a slim dress belt with two sections, each of which will hold just two bills folded lengthwise four times. Does that limit me to just $400? Not at all, since for this purpose (emergency only) I carry these Canadian bills:

The four bills are worth (at the current exchange rate) $2,600. Lately, these money belts have been disappearing from both men's stores and travel shops. I do not know why. You may have to search for them, or have them custom-made at a leather shop.

As for outdoor mildew and rustproof storage, nothing beats silver and gold. I like used American silver dollars, and new Canadian Maple Leaf coins are even better. These one-ounce gold coins currently sell for about $35 over the spot price of gold, and can be scattered about in very small hiding places indeed. One hundred eight thousand dollars Maple Leaf coins can be stuffed into a coffee can, in which case you'd have a "medium"-sized item to hide. However, since gold pays no interest and there are dealer commissions in both buying and selling, holding a large quantity of coins has its disadvantages.

Medium: My principal items in this category are reference books in the fields of scanning, hacking, vanishing, and doing business in the underground economy. Should my wife and I both die in an accident, I do not care to have these come to light. It's a nuisance, but I keep these—plus tax records—off the premises in private storage. (In case of death, a friend of total confidence will clean out the unit and destroy all contents.)

Large: A fireproof file cabinet and a fireproof safe are stored in another location. I do not have a mistress to hide, nor have I arranged a hiding place for my wife and myself. We both are confident that between our almost-invisible profile and the security devices in place, we are not in danger. All the more so since we have no known enemies. (If that should ever change, I do have something in mind.)

Nevertheless, a secret room can give you added security, especially if you are the wife of a traveling man who leaves you home alone. We discovered one new home with an unusual "extra" purely by accident while traveling from Las Vegas to Portland in 1994. On the way (I won't say where, for a reason that will become obvious), my wife wanted to check out a certain rural upscale holiday-home development. The builder included an astonishing list of electronic items as "standard," not the least of which was a soundproof room with a complete home movie theater system with seating for twenty. But there was something more, not shown in the brochures. The agent showing us the model home saved the master bedroom for last. After showing us the "his" and "hers" bathrooms (à la Harrah's at Lake Tahoe), we were shown "his" walk-in closet, then "hers." At this point the agent, a gray-haired overweight lady who sparkled with what must have been zircons in view of the size, asked us if we'd seen the *entire* home.

"Yes," said my wife, "we've seen it all."

"Actually, you haven't," she said, and with that she gave a firm push to the door-sized shoe rack at the far end of the closet.

The shoe rack swung back on oiled offset hinges to reveal a secret room. It was about nine feet square and lined on two sides with storage shelves. There were no windows, but I noticed a vent for the heating system, and a telephone jack on one wall.

"Would you care to comment," I asked her, "on the purpose of this room?"

"No, we call this our *'don't ask, don't tell'* room."

I pass this idea on to you as worthy of consideration when you plan your next new home. The only hesitation I'd have would be that the secret room would be common knowledge among the architect, the contractor, and the workers. Also, the building plans would be on file with the city or county. Gone are the days when pirates buried treasures in deep holes, then murdered the men who'd done the work.

To close this section I'll mention a way to hide whatever-sized item you have in a way that not even Janet Reno nor the ATF can track down. This is a method you've never seen in any book:

1. Put some film in your camera, borrow a fifty-foot or hundred-foot tape measure and purchase a handheld Global Positioning System (GPS) and a compass at any marine store.

2. Go to a "trackless" state-owned desert wilderness (first choice: central Nevada), and look for a distinctive rock in a slightly raised area, to avoid any problem with a flash flood.

3. Carefully take a reading on the rock itself, using the GPS receiver. Write down the precise latitude and longitude. Take pictures of the rock.

4. Bury your container a certain distance away, and note the distance and the magnetic compass direction.

5. With your will, leave instructions. For extra security, give the latitude to your sister Josie, without telling her what the number represents. Then, in your will, you can describe the rock, the exact container location, and the precise longitude. Tell the executor, "Ask my sister Josie for the secret number I gave her." This is the latitude. (And

without the latitude, your cache will be safe. Wouldn't Captain Kidd have liked to have a working GPS!)

The GPS will put the finder within seventy-five feet of the rock, the picture will identify the rock, the compass will indicate the correct magnetic direction, and the tape measure will bring the searcher to the "X" that marks the spot.

By the way, neglecting to put these instructions in your will, and then getting Alzheimer's, would be uncool.

QUESTIONS & ANSWERS

What do you think about buying gold coins and burying them?

Before I answer that, note this gem from *California Lawyer:*

> Texas attorney Scott Erikson pleaded guilty to laundering nearly $3.4 million from two Resolution Trust institutions after authorities found a hand-drawn treasure map in his home that led them to $1 million in buried gold coins bought with some of the stolen money.

He knew enough to hide the coins, but not enough to hide the map. This reminds me of those with secret overseas bank accounts who keep the bank statements at home. By the way, a million in gold weighs about 250 pounds. That alone might discourage me from trading cash for gold. But if you want to bury just a few dozen pounds, well, why not? Just make sure you hide the map as well as you hide the coins.

20

COOL STUFF THAT DID NOT FIT IN EARLIER

Come, Watson, come! The game is afoot. Not a word!
Into your clothes and come!

—SIR ARTHUR CONAN DOYLE,
"THE ADVENTURE OF THE ABBEY GRANGE"

If Sherlock Holmes were alive today, he would not have to leave
his rented first-floor flat at 220B Baker Street, London. Instead,
he would be sitting at his computer, breaking into confidential
databases. If that did not produce results, then he would turn to
the telephone and make "pretext" calls.

My dictionary says a pretext is "a purpose or motive alleged
or an appearance assumed in order to cloak the real intention or
state of affairs." Private investigators push this meaning to the
outermost limits. Complete books have been and are being written for private detectives, showing them how to obtain any information whatsoever. Here is a typical example of how a
pretext works.

For a brief time, Karl and Lorelei are lovers. When Karl
turns violent, Lorelei walks out. Karl stalks her. She moves

away and rents a room in a private hotel under another name. Karl can no longer track her down so he goes to Guido, a PI known for getting results where others fail. He tells Guido a made-up sob story and the PI does not bother to check it out. He takes a hefty retainer from Karl and writes down what scanty information Karl has—her full name, Social Security number, former address, and the name of a hospital where she was once briefly admitted.

The PI promises Karl results in ten days. Actually, Guido will have Lorelei's new address within the hour, obtained with just two short "pretext" telephone calls. The first is to Plano General Hospital.

> *PGH:*   Hello, please hold. [long pause]
>
> *PGH:*   Plano General Hospital, may I help you?
>
> *Guido:*   Yes, This is John, with Dr. Childress's office in McKinney, and I'm processing some insurance forms for Lorelei Altbusser. Could you pull that file for me? I need the date of admission.
>
> *PGH:*   Do you have her Social Security number?
>
> *Guido:*   Let's see [makes sound of papers shuffling]. Yeah, it's 987-65-4325.
>
> *PGH:*   OK, please hold for a minute while I get the file. [pause]
>
> *PGH:*   OK, got it. She was admitted 10-10-99.
>
> *Guido:*   What was the complaint?
>
> *PGH:*   Looks like persistent pains following a recent abortion.
>
> *Guido:*   Does it indicate any treatment?
>
> *PGH:*   Looks like there was a prescription, that was all.
>
> *Guido:*   Well, thanks for the help, and—oh, one more thing. On the form she filled out, does it list her mother's name as Mary Altbusser, with telephone 344-1288?
>
> *PGH:*   No, her admittance form lists next of kin as Gertrude Altbusser at 478-1991.
>
> *Guido:*   *Muchas gracias, and have a nice day.*

Next, the PI calls 478-1991 because he figures Lorelei keeps in contact with her mother. Once again, he represents himself as a doctor.

Guido: Gertrude Altbusser, please.

Mother: Yes, this is she.

Guido: Mrs. Altbusser, this is Dr. Noe at the Cook County Morgue. We have a body here that's been tentatively identified as a Lorelei Altbusser. Do you have a daughter by that name?

Mother: *Oh, my God! Oh no! Oh God!*

Guido: Mrs. Altbusser, is your daughter an African-American?

Mother: *No, no, my daughter is white!*

   [Guido's reason for whipsawing this poor woman back and forth is to inject her with truth serum. Now she will tell him what he wants to know.]

Guido: Mrs. Altbusser, how do you explain this dead black girl having your daughter's driver's license?

Mother: I don't know. Maybe Lorelei's purse was stolen?

Guido: Mrs. Altbusser, when's the last time you spoke with your daughter?

Mother: I talked to her last Sunday. She's a good girl, she calls me every Sunday.

Guido: Mrs. Altbusser, it's very important we speak with your daughter on this matter without delay. How can I get in touch with her immediately?

Mother: "She's renting a room in Odessa now, and doesn't have a telephone, but I do have the number at a Circle K, where she works. Would you like that number?"

Guido: Yes, please give it to me now, ma'am.

Mother: It's 960-362-0464.

Guido: Thank you, Mrs. Altbusser.

One PI, writing about the above pretext, does add this word of caution: "When using the Dead Black Female routine, mothers of the girl you are looking for may become hysterical. I've heard of cases where the mother has literally dropped the phone in mid-sentence and raced over to the county morgue. . . ."

PRIVATE INVESTIGATORS—FRIENDS OR FOES?

In the foregoing example, from Lorelei's viewpoint, the PI was just a miserable Liar for Hire. (However, shall we give that story a happy ending? Karl drives to Odessa, locates Lorelei, and starts waving a handgun. She kicks him in the groin, takes his gun away, and plugs him through the heart.) But let's change the context. Suppose the one who goes to the PI is *you*, and Lorelei is *your* daughter. She just turned sixteen and ran off to Chicago with some guy named Armen Bedrosian who is twice her age. You call the Cook County Police but you think you are getting a runaround. You go to a PI who checks Armen out via the Internet and tells you the man is an ex-con who was jailed in his teens for rape and attempted murder. He has only been back on the streets for two months. The PI tracks Armen down by first locating his mother. He calls her.

"Mrs. Bedrosian, this is Dr. Noe at the Cook County Morgue. We have a body here that's been tentatively identified as Armen Bedrosian. Do you have a son by that name?"

If the PI saves your teenage daughter, will you not bless his efforts to the end of your days?

Are all PIs competent? No more than all lawyers are competent. As in any other profession there are experts, and there are those that just bumble through. Consider the following two cases.

THE ELLEN DEVER CASE

April 10, 1999, was "family day" for Ellen Dever, forty-four, and her daughters Genevieve, seven, and Sarah, nine. After lunch at a sidewalk café in Lucerne, Switzerland, they bought magazines and shopped for sunglasses. Then they strolled along the street, eating ice cream and talking about Sarah's first Holy Communion, which was scheduled for the following day.

Someone had been out to get Ellen's daughters for the past two years and that someone was their millionaire father. When he had attempted to get sole custody of the girls, Ellen sold her five-hundred-thousand-dollar home in Radnor Township, Pennsylvania, and fled with the girls to Belgium. From there they moved to Greece and a month later, under aliases, they arrived in Lucerne, where Ellen rented a comfortable apartment that was part of a larger house.

Ellen, fearful that her ex-husband might someday track her down, started taking jujitsu lessons. Little by little, however, her fears faded. The girls attended the local Montessori school, had ballet lessons, and took classes in art. By then, they were fluent in German and Italian as well as in English.

Genevieve stopped to take a drink from a fountain, and Sarah kidded her about her missing tooth, which had fallen out the previous week. Ellen reminded herself that she had done everything right. A new country, new names, no contact with the past. And then she spotted two men watching her from a distance up ahead. They looked like Bad Guys right out of the movies, wearing huge sunglasses and hats with the brims pulled down. They were built like linebackers.

"Let's go!" she told the girls, hurrying them back toward their apartment. Within minutes, the two men Ellen had seen suddenly appeared before her, and a third man came up behind. As the men reached for the girls, Ellen attacked them with every jujitsu blow she could muster. At the same time a white van with tinted windows screeched to a stop alongside them, and the girls were manhandled into the van, fighting every step of the way. The side door was slammed shut and the van sped off, leaving a bleeding Ellen behind, clutching one of the men's blue-and-beige hat.

How had she been found?

Not by the police or the FBI. Not by the one hundred bounty hunters that had been searching for her ever since the ex-husband offered a $2 million reward. She was found by one of the private investigators that her husband had hired on four continents.

THE BARBARA KURTH FAGAN CASE

Stephen and Barbara Fagan had been married for five years, eloping to Haiti on the day that Stephen divorced Leah, his first wife. Then came a venomous divorce. He got the house. She got the kids. He didn't like that, and on October 28, 1979, he snatched the children, then only two and five, from his ex-wife's home in suburban Boston. He fled with the girls to Palm Beach County, Florida, where his parents and a sister already lived. He changed the girls' names to Rachael and Lisa and his own to William Stephen Martin.

Back in Massachusetts, Barbara regained her maiden name of Kurth and filed a criminal complaint. Over the years, she hired various private investigators, but they came up blank. Finally, she gave up. She pressed ahead with her own life, remarried, and became a noted expert in cell biology.

Meanwhile, her ex-husband fashioned a good life for himself in south Florida. Big houses, fast cars, and very rich wives. Nearly twenty years passed before someone in his or his latest wife's family decided Fagan's days of high living should come to an end. A tip to the authorities was all it took. Police nabbed him at his $2.2-million-dollar oceanfront estate, bought by wife number four, and he was returned to Massachusetts to face felony charges of kidnapping.

Why couldn't Stephen Fagan's wife track him down? One reason is given in the May 25, 1998 issue of *Newsweek*:

> Fagan and his daughters insist Kurth should have been
> able to find them if she'd really searched. Kurth's family

says she spent more than $10,000 on lawyers and private
investigators—to no avail. A 1982 report from one PI
warns her that staking out Fagan's sister's home in Florida
would be an expensive long shot.

Others say she spent triple that but whatever it was, either it
was not enough, or she hired the wrong investigators. PIs like
Robert Scott, Norma Tillman, Patrick Picciarelli, Fay Faron, or
Leigh Hearon charge from $95 to $150 an hour, but they may
be the cheapest in the long run. I quote from an e-mail I received
from Norma Tillman, author of *How to Find Almost Anyone,
Anywhere:*

Fagan should have been located easily. I worked in law-
enforcement 11 years and when detectives couldn't find
their suspect they would give it to me. One time a detective was looking for a brutal serial rapist. He really wanted
to catch him. I was at home about to bake a cake when
he called and asked me to help him find the suspect. I put
the cake in the oven and found the offender before the
cake was done. The detective received "Officer of the
Year" for capturing him.

Private investigator John J. Nazarian says that success depends
on two things: "How much you want to spend, and how you
want to play the game. . . ."

A CLUE (?) TO A TRUSTWORTHY PI

This question once came up: All other things being equal, which
kind of PI would you be more likely to trust—a man or a
woman?

I am not going to alienate half my readers by giving a personal
opinion. Instead, I shall merely quote the first four paragraphs
from a long article in the *Los Angeles Times* datelined August 3,

1999, and titled POLICE CHIEF PUTS THE BRAKES ON
MEXICO CITY'S TRAFFIC COPS. Read the following and
draw your own conclusions.

> *Mexico City:* Imagine a corruption problem so serious that
> you don't trust your traffic cops to give out tickets.
>
> Mexico City Police Chief Alejandro Gertz faced a
> public outcry over exactly that dilemma. So Monday, he
> took away all the citation books from the city's 900 traffic
> officers.
>
> Instead, Gertz authorized just 30 police cars—each
> staffed by two policewomen, who are deemed less cor-
> ruptible—to issue traffic tickets. The other traffic cops will
> be restricted to directing the capital's perpetually snarled
> traffic.
>
> In announcing the plan last week, Gertz said residents
> of the Federal District—home to 8.5 million people and
> nearly 3 million registered vehicles—were so fed up with
> paying bribes to traffic police that he had no choice but
> to stop the officers from handing out tickets.

WHO ARE THE "PT" PEOPLE?

The initials "PT" are used to describe an estimated five hundred
thousand European residents (which includes American expatri-
ates) who have a certain state of mind that is different from that
of you and me. The term originated with Harry Schultz, of *Guin-
ness Book of Records* fame ("World's Highest Paid Consultant"),
and author of the *International Harry Schultz Letter.* Harry, originally from Milwaukee, was a boy wonder in the newspaper industry but, disillusioned with Americans' growing penchant for
suing one another, took off to see the world in the 1960s and
never returned as a permanent U.S. resident.

PT can stand for anything from *Part-time* to *Perpetual Tourist.*
The hard-core PT considers himself a part-time resident of var-

ious countries but a taxpaying citizen of none, since in whatever country he finds himself, he is just "Passing Through." I suspect Harry himself is not hard-core, but I've met plenty who are.

One of them was Wolfgang Winkler, who was born in Switzerland, lives in London, has an office in Singapore, does business in the United States, and keeps his money in an unknown country. (First he paid me with thousand-dollar money orders from Barclays, later with cash in hundred-dollar bills, and the last time he neglected to pay me at all, which ended our arrangement.)

Winkler serves as substitute (i.e., nominee) director for some 2,500 international corporations secretly owned by fellow PT clients, and—back when we were still on speaking terms—educated me on the extent of the PT phenomenon.

"I've got some *very* rich clients," he told me one foggy afternoon over tea at London's Inn on the Park, "who have never paid one penny, franc, or lira in income taxes in the past fifteen years."

One of these clients, who shall not here be named, I know quite well. The following details about this person are typical of thousands of PTs:

1. He was born in Germany but emigrated at age twenty-eight thus getting off the tax rolls in Germany, as he was "officially" moving to South Africa, where he would take up permanent residence. *He never arrived.*

2. He obtained a driver's license from the UK, since it could be done by mail and the license did not contain a picture. (This may have changed in recent years.)

3. He purchased a tourist-trap bar and club in Andorra through a resident nominee, and brought in a cousin to run it.

4. He bought a "holiday home" from me in the Canary Islands and paid me with a shopping bag full of dollars, pounds, francs, and D marks.

5. He travels extensively and owns rental properties in Las Vegas.

6. He banks in Gibraltar, and has a safe-deposit box in Guernsey in the Channel Islands.

7. In no country of the world does he pay taxes, since wherever he may happen to be he's just "passing through."

I do not subscribe to the PT mentality, and neither should you, but this does not preclude learning basic principles. Applying them, you may wish to:

(a) Arrange to have your legal domicile (which will be your ghost address) in New Hampshire (no state sales tax, no state income tax). If you are a voter, this is the state where you will cast your vote for the least-worst candidates in each election.

(b) Own a "second home" in California, which will actually be your true residence.

(c) Run an invisible business based in Pioche, Nevada.

(d) Domicile the corporation used in Pioche in tax-free Wyoming (to avoid the frequent-audit problem with Nevada corporations).

(e) Title your Lincoln LS with an LLC and obtain license plates from both New Hampshire and California.

If you follow all these steps, PT might stand for Pretty Thorough. (It might also violate a law or two in California so consider the ramifications carefully.)

SNEAK-AND-PEEK WARRANTS

(Based on the *FBI Law Enforcement Bulletin*, February 1997) I checked this one out with several attorneys, who tell me this is one item they never heard about in law school. Basically, law-enforcement officers can obtain a sneak-and-peek warrant "when there is a legitimate need for the government to covertly uncover information that could not be obtained through other, more traditional means of investigation." Once obtained, the warrants are to be used within seven days. They are just as the name implies. Officers will enter surreptitiously and search for evidence that could later be the basis for a normal search warrant. The victim will almost never know an entry has been made.

HOW TO DEAL WITH CLERKS AND TELLERS

First of all, dress like they do, or just a bit better. *Source:* John J. Molloy, *Dress for Success*. No matter how convinced you are that clothes make the man or woman, reading John J. Molloy's best-seller, *Dress for Success*, will make you even more of a true believer. To Molloy's book I add the following: If you are a woman, dress and act like a woman, emphasis on "dress" as in the noun. If you are a man, and if getting others to accept your requests for privacy is high on your list of priorities, show up freshly shaved and with a recent short haircut. *Source:* Me. Right or wrong, I often refuse requests from anyone who draws attention to himself or herself by outward appearance rather than by inward qualities of honesty, integrity, loyalty, and virtue. (I wish they'd teach that in grade schools.)

Next, when at all possible, *deal with the opposite sex*. This applies to trips to the bank, the county courthouse, the utility companies, and to any other location where low-level clerks deal with the public. If you are a woman, seek out a man. If you are a man, talk to a woman. *Source*: innumerable private investigators.

HOW TO DELAY THE SERVING OF A SUBPOENA

A subpoena is an order, usually signed by a notary public, to attend a legal proceeding such as a trial or deposition. A subpoena *duces tectum*—Latin for "bring with you"—means you are

ordered to bring certain documents with you, which can be anything from bank statements to old love letters. The purpose of a
subpoena is to force you to produce something you do not want
to produce, and/or to appear in a civil or criminal court case
when that is on the very bottom of your "things-I'd-like-to-do"
list. Although it is not correct to say that if they can't find you
they can't serve you, this process certainly can, and often should
be, delayed as long as possible, thus giving you time to think
things out.

(At this late date, don't do a Nixon and erase tapes, nor an
Ollie North and shred documents. If your tape, document, or
photo files need work, stop reading NOW and start erasing,
burning, flushing, burying, encrypting, and shredding *before* the
storm clouds gather.)

In a civil case, a subpoena can be delivered by a law-firm
employee, a professional process server, peace officer, or anyone
else of legal age (in some countries, registered and bonded) capable of making multiple attempts, able to correctly fill out the
proof or certificate of service, and who can testify as a credible
witness if the service is challenged.

In a criminal case, service will be achieved if you acknowledge
receipt of the subpoena by telephone or mail, as well as in person. The way you identify yourself (should you ever want to . . .)
is by name, date of birth, and driver's license number.

Delaying service of a subpoena is not for amateurs. Beyond a
certain point, if it can be shown that you *willfully* disobeyed it,
the court can issue a bench warrant for your arrest. Now is the
time to call in an experienced shark, preferably of the species
great white, bull, tiger, or oceanic whitetip. This lawyer will
know many sneaky tricks about *serving* subpoenas and will thus
be able to tell you how and up to what point you can delay
service.

Now then, if service appears to be inevitable, at least take
control of *where* and *when* this is to happen. Don't get caught
unaware like Franklin K——from Cleveland. He owed his lawyer
money but he had a daughter's wedding coming up, so he chose

to stall the lawyer and throw an elaborate wedding reception. The lawyer learned about this and decided to cause the greatest humiliation possible to his delinquent client.

At the precise moment Franklin stood up to propose a toast to the new bride and groom, the sheriff barged in and served Franklin with a subpoena! Learn from this and if you fear you will be served with a subpoena, do not attend a public gathering where you may be known, and do not admit your identity to a stranger.

If you *are* served, have your legal beagle bring a motion to quash. (You may have heard that the process server must touch your face or body with the papers. Not true; he can just toss the papers at your feet, or whatever.) Have him claim that service was improper and statutory requirements were not met.

> *When uncertain,*
> *Or in doubt,*
> *Run in circles!*
> *Scream and shout!*

21

AN EXAM, A SECRET, AND AN INVITATION

And life is what we make it. Always has been, always will be.

—Grandma Moses

What follows is a true story, outlined in *Street Sense for Students* by Louis R. Mizell, Jr. A private investigator ran up a bill of $3,000 on this case without a single positive result. You, however, having read this book, are now equipped to solve the mystery.

Ready?

FINAL EXAM

Becky was a twenty-nine-year-old medical student living alone in an off-campus residence. Her telephone was listed in another name. She received the first call from a stalker at three in the morning.

"I follow you everywhere," he said. "I know your most intimate thoughts." He then proceeded to tell her things that no one else could have known.

Two nights later, he called again. "Becky, I saw you buying eggs and pancake mix at the Super Giant yesterday. How did you know that's what I like for breakfast?" Another night, he called to ask her when she was going to show him "the bra and panties *we* bought at Neiman Marcus."

Everything the man said was true, but how did he know? Becky had been constantly on the watch for anyone who was following her but had seen nothing suspicious.

She went to the police, who were unable to help her. Worse, they steered her to an incompetent PI who took her money but did not help her. She changed her telephone to another name—unlisted—and for a while the calls ceased. Then, three days before Christmas, the telephone rang at two in the morning.

"I wish you'd get a female doctor—I don't like Dr. Johnson looking at my lady. Next time *I'll* give you a physical."

Increasingly distraught, Becky flew home to be with her family over the holidays. On Christmas morning, while the family was unwrapping gifts, the telephone rang. Becky's mother answered. The caller asked to speak to Becky. When she came on the line, he said, "I'd like to unwrap you right now." She broke down and cried.

Are you ready to solve the mystery? To assist you, here is some additional information:

- The stalker never watched her or followed her.
- He had no accomplices.
- He did not bug her car or her apartment.
- He did not tap her telephone.
- He did not clean her cordless telephone or her cell phone.
- He did not use a computer in any way.

- He did not contact anyone that knew her.
- He did not steal mail from her mailbox.
- He did not get information about her from any other person.

Desperate, Becky went to a security company. When she described the problems she had been having, they recognized a certain pattern and—unlike the PI who charged $3,000—they guessed the answer on the spot. All they had to do now was prove it.

They hid a camera near Becky's driveway and had an off-duty police officer monitor it from inside a van parked nearby. Just after 4 A.M., a man parked a Volkswagen nearby. He then picked up Becky's trash and emptied it into a plastic garbage bag he had brought along.

The next item to be picked up was the thirty-one-year-old man. He turned out to have prior convictions for burglary, drug, and sex crimes and had failed to report to his parole officer. All his information had come from Becky's unshredded trash.

- Cash-register receipts showed all of her purchases.
- Her phone numbers came from discarded telephone bills.
- The doctor's name was on an empty prescription-drug container.
- The rest of the information came from other things Becky had thrown away: personal letters, class schedules, notes, and bills.

THE SECRET INGREDIENT

None of the information in this book will be of assistance to you unless you put the suggestions into practice. I urge you to start *now.* Do not wait until you can find the time—you may never find it. Do not wait until you can "do it right," because that day may never come.

All successful persons can list one or more secrets for success. My entrepreneurial father passed on his own two secrets of success to me when I left home to seek my way in the world. ("To make money, you must go where the money is," and "Never take a partner.") Earl Nightingale wrote an entire best-selling book with a single theme, *The Strangest Secret.* ("We become what we think about.")

Well, *my* secret isn't very strange. In fact, it's so obvious that I fear you will disregard it:

> *For every desired action, set a date, and when the date arrives, just go ahead and do it. NO MATTER WHAT.*

My rule does not have any rhythm to it, it doesn't even rhyme, but it works for me and it will work for you. Here is the application: Make a list of what you wish to accomplish and *set a date* to complete each item. And when the time comes, just do it. Decide on your level of privacy, then write down the suggestions you plan to follow and set a date for their completion. Your goal is never again to have your true name coupled with your true address. Here is a short review:

- Obtain at least one ghost address and give this to your out-of-town relatives, friends, banks, insurance companies, utility companies, IRS, DMV, and everyone else.
- Disconnect your present telephone. Then have it reconnected in another name. Get a cell phone in another name.
- Order new checks for your bank account from a mail-order company and do not list your name on the checks, nor any address. Start with a high number.

- If you use e-mail, change to one of the free services such as hushmail.com or Stribmail.com and be discreet when filling in the application blanks.
- If you are renting, move. If you are a homeowner, sell, then start over.
- Find a nominee. Order one or more LLCs so they will be on hand when you suddenly need them.
- Start an invisible home-based business if you have not already done so.
- Travel with a lower profile. Practice crossing into Canada and Mexico. Look at every challenge to your privacy as an adventure. Get a life, have fun during the day, sleep without worries at night.

As this book goes to press, it is as up-to-date as I can make it. However, some changes may have taken place before you have this book in your hands. If you have access to the Internet, you may wish to check *www.howtobeinvisible.com* for any updated information. The password is ssndob, short for *Social Security number–date of birth.*

If you have any comments or suggestions, I would be happy to hear from you. When you address your letter, please do not start out with "J. J. Luna." Rather, address it using four lines in this exact order:

Marrero and Luna
Apartado de Correos, 2
35626 Morro del Jable, LP de GC
Canary Islands, Spain

Although I do not have the time to answer letters personally, all will be read. The best ideas will be incorporated into future editions of this book.

Finally, if you remember nothing else, remember this: *Do not, as long as you live, ever again allow your real name to be coupled with your home address.* If you commit this to memory and put it into practice, then you will be well on your way to invisibility.

Yours faithfully,
J. J. Luna
Fuerteventura Island
Winter 2002

GLOSSARY

Aka or a.k.a.: "Also known as"

CMRA: Commercial mail-receiving agency. More commonly known as a "mail drop."

CPA: Certified Public Accountant.

IRS: Internal Revenue Service.

LLC: A limited-liability company.

Mail drop: An address other than your own where you can receive mail, packages, and courier deliveries.

Ghost address: A future address you will use that has no connection to where you really live.

NSA: The National Security Agency.

PI: Private investigator or private eye. Sometimes used to referred to a private detective, although the use of the word "detective" is prohibited in some states and many countries. (In the Netherlands, for example, the title "Detective" refers to a PI who is working illegally without a license!)

SSN: Social Security number.

DOB: Date of birth.

APPENDIX

PERSONAL RECOMMENDATIONS

I have no financial interest in any of the following publications. The magazine and the newsletter are merely the ones I read first when they arrive in the mail, and the book is the one I have underlined and refer to more than any other.

P.I. Magazine ("America's Private Investigation Journal"), 755 Bronx, Toledo, Ohio 43609. Phone/fax 419-382-0967. E-mail: *PIMaga1@aol.com*. See at *www.PIMag.com*.

This magazine is published every other month ($39 per year) for private investigators. Both the articles and the advertisements are oriented toward tracking down people who do not wish to be found. I read it, of course, to find out what the latest tricks are for the opposition and then dream up ways to foil them.

E-mail: intelligence@earthlink.net. Web: www.intelligence.to. This is an eight-page newsletter for private investigators, published ten times a year. The annual subscription rate is $109. The editor uses the name "Lee Lapin." Each issue usually contains a number of interesting Web sites. The most interesting one I've run across so far is *www.searchgateway.com*. This site will lead you to international databases for looking up persons by name and/or address. It also has reverse searches for obtaining names from telephone numbers or addresses, plus many other interesting links.

Stopping a Stalker: A Cop's Guide to Making the System Work for You, by Captain Robert L. Snow (Plenum Press, 1998, 265 pages). If you think stopping a stalker is easy, this book will change your mind. Snow cites one account in which a stalker went through the computer files of his target's home computer. In another case, a stalker burglarized his target's parent's home near San Francisco in order to obtain her current address in Los

Angeles. (Warning: This is not a good book to read when you are home alone on a dark and stormy night.)

Private Investigators: If you wish to track someone down, there is no better place to start than with Patrick Picciarelli:
    Telephone (724) 684-8184
    Fax (724) 684-7476
    Website: http://www.dp.net/~condor/PI. (The URL is case sensitive and should be typed as indicated.)

New Mexico Limited Liability Companies: The address below is that of a young lady who charges only $99 to form a new LLC, and only $99 per year for the New Mexico resident agent. Despite the faraway address, she responds with lightning speed. Be sure to mark your letter AIRMAIL and add 80 cents for overseas postage. Or, if you have e-mail, contact her at canaryislands@hushmail.com.

    M.M.M. (Valterra)
    C/Benito Perez Armas, 12
    35500 Arrecife de Lanzarote
    Canary Islands, Spain

This coupon is for a
FREE UPDATE!

I reserve the right to limit this offer to the first five thousand requests received, so please send in your requests promptly. If you also wish to receive information about New Mexico limited liability companies, check the box at the bottom.

Privacy statement: Your name and address will be kept confidential. It will not be sold, rented, or given to any third party.

Disclaimer: This offer for a free update is made by me personally, and will be sent out at my expense. There is no connection between this offer and St. Martin's Press, nor will St. Martin's Press profit in any way. *Note*: I am in my seventies as this book goes to press. If I die before the coupon comes in . . . I will not send you any update!

Please fill out this form so that—if still alive—I can mail you the free update on this book. Address your envelope *exactly* as shown below.

Name _____   *Mail to*:
                                  M.M.M. (Valterra)
Address _____   C/Benito Perez Armas, 12
                                  35500 Arrecife de Lanzarote
         _____   Canary Islands, SPAIN

IMPORTANT: You must send this ORIGINAL coupon.
Photo copies will not be accepted.

☐ Please include free information about
low-cost limited liability companies.

INDEX

ABOUT THE AUTHOR

In the 1950s, J. J. Luna sold his outdoor advertising business in North Dakota and moved with his wife and small children to the Canary Islands off the coast of West Africa. Outwardly, he was a professional photographer. Secretly, he worked underground in an activity that was at that time illegal under the regime of Generalissimo Francisco Franco.

In 1970 Franco, yielding to intense pressure from the Western World, moderated Spain's laws, leaving Luna free to come in from the cold. By that time, however, privacy had become an ingrained habit. In the years that followed he started up various low-profile businesses, built them up, then sold them. He is currently an international consultant specializing in personal privacy and security.